D0887105

INFLUENTIAL
L!VES

CRISTIANO RONALDO

INTERNATIONAL SOCCER STAR

David Fischer

Enslow Publishing
101 W. 23rd Street
Suite 240
New York, NY 10011
USA

enslow.com

Published in 2019 by Enslow Publishing, LLC.
101 W. 23rd Street, Suite 240, New York, NY 10011

Library of Congress Cataloging-in-Publication Data

Title: Cristiano Ronaldo / David Fischer.
Description: New York : Enslow Publishing, 2019. | Series: Influential Lives
| Includes bibliographical references and index. | Audience: Grades: 7-12.
Identifiers: LCCN 2017018596 | ISBN 9780766092051 (library bound) | ISBN 9781978501713 (paperback)
Subjects: LCSH: Ronaldo, Cristiano, 1985—Juvenile literature. | Soccer
players—Portugal—Biography—Juvenile literature.
Classification: LCC GV942.7.R626 F57 2018 | DDC 796.334092 [B] —dc23
LC record available at https://lccn.loc.gov/2017018596

Printed in the United States of America

To Our Readers: We have done our best to make sure all websites in this book were active and appropriate when we went to press. However, the author and the publisher have no control over and assume no liability for the material available on those websites or on any websites they may link to. Any comments or suggestions can be sent by e-mail to customerservice@enslow.com.

Photo credits: Cover, p. 1 Michael Buholzer/AFP/Getty Images; p. 4 Quinn Rooney/Getty Images; p. 9 Roger Eritja/Alamy Stock Photo; p. 13 Angel Martinez/Real Madrid/Getty Images; pp. 19, 23, 6(AFP/Getty Images; p. 27 Patricia De Melo Moreira/AFP/Getty Images; p. 31 VI-Images/Getty Images; pp. 36, 45 Antonio Cotrim/AFP/Getty Images; p. 41 Estela Silva/AFP/Getty Images; p. 49 John Peters/Manchester United/Getty Images; p. 53 Alex Livesey/Getty Images; pp. 56, 65 Adrian Dennis, AFP/Getty Images; p. 70 Denis Doyle/Getty Images; p. 73 Twocoms/Shutterstock.com; p. 75 © AP Images; p. 81 Paul Ellis/AFP/Getty Images; p. 85 Pierre-Philippe Marcou/AFP/Getty Images; p. 86 Sonny Tumbelaka/AFP/Getty Images; p. 91 Philipp Schmidli/Getty Images; p. 96 Anadolu Agency/ Getty Images; p. 101 Gregorio Cunha/AFP/Getty Images; p. 104 Lars Baron/Getty Images; back cover and interior pages background graphic zffoto/Shutterstock.com.

Contents

Introduction

T he final match of the 2004 European Championships between Portugal and Greece was expected to end with Portugal finally winning a major international tournament. Before the tournament began, Portugal was considered to be the overwhelming favorite, while the odds on Greece winning were very slim. As expected, the atmosphere at Estádio da Luz, in Lisbon, Portugal, was electric on that July 4 day. Portugal hadn't lost a game on home soil for seventeen years. The entire country was rooting for them, willing them to succeed. But Greece defied all odds and pulled off an upset win, 1–0, which must be regarded as one of the biggest shocks in the history of the sport.

As the final seconds ticked off the clock, nineteen-year-old Portugal star Cristiano Ronaldo burst into tears.

Cristiano Ronaldo celebrates after scoring a goal, a frequent occurrence for the celebrated Portuguese soccer superstar.

With one season of English Premier League football under his belt for Manchester United, Ronaldo was called up for Euro 2004 and had an immediate impact, helping the Portuguese side reach the final. Looking lost and alone at midfield when the final whistle sounded, television cameras caught Ronaldo sobbing uncontrollably, for the world to see. It is a heartbreaking image that will stay in the minds of soccer fans forever.

Perhaps those teenage tears were a result of having missed his best opportunities to score, like in the 59th minute, when a Greek defender thwarted his run into the penalty area, or in the 74th, when he sent an uncontested shot over the bar. Or perhaps he was reduced to tears because of his passion for the game and his unquenchable will to win. To be sure, the crushing and painful loss shattered him to the core, as his dream of winning a trophy for Portugal was quashed.

Ronaldo has been criticized throughout his life for his tendency to cry during tough times. This has been seen by some as a sign of weakness. Sometimes, however, crying can prove that a human being is alive, as in the case of a newborn baby taking its first breaths. And Cristiano Ronaldo is never more alive than when he's on the soccer field trying to lead his team to victory.

After that devastating loss in Euro 2004, Ronaldo said, "Now I have to move on. I have to look forward. There will be many other opportunities to win in Europe throughout my career, and make up for this huge disappointment."[1]

Since then, Ronaldo has matured to the point where he has become one of the most decorated players in the sport. The success he enjoys has come from years of hard work and sacrifice that have helped him overcome many obstacles and difficulties in his path. It is hard to imagine one of the world's best players facing adversity as a youngster. But knowing what he has gone through makes Cristiano Ronaldo's rise to the top even more impressive.

CHAPTER ONE

Poor Kid from the Island

· · · · · · · · · · · · ·

Cristiano Ronaldo was born on February 5, 1985, in the Santo António neighborhood of Funchal, the capital city of Madeira, a small island in the Atlantic Ocean a few hundred miles south of Portugal. His father, José Dinis Aveiro, known to friends as Dinis, worked as a gardener for the city, and his mother, Maria Dolores dos Santos, who went by Dolores, worked as a cook and a housekeeper in other people's homes. Cristiano is the youngest of four children. He has one older brother, Hugo, and two older sisters, Elma and Liliana Cátia.

The given name on his birth certificate is Cristiano Ronaldo dos Santos Aveiro. It is a Portuguese tradition that when a child is born, he receives both parents' surnames: the family name of the mother followed by the last name of the father. The name Ronaldo was added to honor Ronald Reagan, who was the president of the United States at the time of Cristiano's birth. Dinis and Dolores did not have politics on their mind when they chose the middle name Ronaldo for their youngest child; it was because Ronald Reagan was his parents' favorite Hollywood film actor. Reagan had starred in American cowboy movies before he entered politics, and those Western-themed films showcasing the Wild West were popular all around world.

"My sister, who was working in an orphanage at the time, said that if [our baby] was a boy we could name him Cristiano," recalled Dolores. "I thought it was a good choice. And my husband and I both liked the name

An aerial view of Cristiano Ronaldo's hometown, Funchal, the capital city of Madeira. The island is a popular vacation spot, famous for its Madeira wine, near-perfect climate, beautiful beaches, and luxurious hotels enjoyed by tourists year-round.

Ronaldo, after Ronald Reagan. My sister chose Cristiano and we chose Ronaldo."[1]

Sign from Above

Cristiano was a big baby. At birth, he was nearly 20½ inches (52 centimeters) long and weighed 9 pounds (4 kilograms). His parents were devoted to the Roman Catholic religion. When it came time for the boy to be baptised, Cristiano's parents scheduled the ceremony to be held at the church in Santo António, but his father's love of soccer nearly spoiled the special occasion. In addition to his gardening duties for the town of Funchal, Dinis earned extra money by working as the equipment

The Gipper

Ronald Reagan (1911–2004), a former actor and governor of California, served as the fortieth president of the United States, from 1981 to 1989. At age sixty-nine, he was the oldest person elected to the presidency until Donald Trump was elected at age seventy in 2016.

Reagan initially chose a career as a Hollywood movie actor, appearing in more than fifty films. Among his best-known roles was that of Notre Dame football star George Gipp in the 1940 biographical film *Knute Rockne All American*. In the movie, Reagan was famous for saying, "Win one for the Gipper."

Reagan, who survived a 1981 assassination attempt only sixty-nine days after his inauguration, died at age ninety-three after battling Alzheimer's disease.

manager for CF Andorinha, one of the local soccer teams based in Santo António.

The baptism was scheduled to begin at the church at six o'clock, but Cristiano's father and godfather, the Andorinha team captain, Fernão Sousa, were already fifteen minutes late. The priest was nervous because another baptism was scheduled to follow immediately after Cristiano's. Dolores was embarrassed. She stalled for time, telling the priest that her husband and the godfather were on their way and would arrive at any minute. But she knew where the men were, and she knew that she could not tell the priest. Not everyone on the island of Madeira was as obsessed with soccer as her family.

Not far from the church, an important game between Andorinha and a local rival was about to end. The game started thirty minutes late, and as Dinis paced the sidelines, he prayed the referee wouldn't add any extra time. Most of all, he hoped the priest would be patient and delay the christening. Finally, Dinis and Fernão dashed into the church, thirty minutes late, rushing to put on their nice clothes over their blue and white Andorinha jerseys. Despite the delay, the baptism of Cristiano Ronaldo dos Santos Aveiro went smoothly. When the ceremony was over and the church photographer was ready to capture the precious moment, Dinis insisted that his infant son be photographed wearing the blue and white colors of his beloved Andorinha team. This picture, one of the earliest photos of Cristiano, is a fitting image for a future soccer superstar.

Cramped Quarters

Cristiano grew up in a poor working-class neighborhood in a small home with no electricity. The only light coming into the home spilled in through the bedroom windows. His parents shared one tiny bedroom, and Cristiano and his brother and sisters shared the other. A third little room was where the family gathered to cook and eat meals together. There was also a bathroom, the size of a broom closet. The home was very cramped for a family of six people. "It was a small space, but I didn't mind," said Ronaldo. "I'm incredibly close with my brother and sisters and we loved being together."[2]

Another flaw of the little house was the dozen or so holes in the tin roof.

There was never enough money to fix it. During Madeira's frequent rainy seasons, a leaky ceiling was a serious problem, as it allowed the wet weather to trickle inside. Cristiano's mother strategically placed cooking pots and drinking cups underneath the dripping water, trying her best to keep the family home as dry as possible. Ronaldo remembers that even though his family was poor, his parents worked hard to give their children a comfortable life. "For us it was normal, it was all we knew," said Ronaldo. "Everyone around us lived the same way and we were happy."[3]

Despite having hard-working parents, Cristiano's family struggled to make ends meet. Although he and his siblings never went hungry, Cristiano knew that his family was poor. His favorite meal was *bacalhau*, a traditional Portuguese dish consisting of salted codfish, potatoes, onions, and scrambled eggs. But there often

The Ronaldo family was and continues to be very close. Above, mother Maria and brother Hugo celebrate the Ballon d'Or with Cristiano and son Cristiano Jr. in 2016.

• • • • • • • • • • • • • • • • • • • •

wasn't enough money to buy the fish, so at those times his mother cooked bacalhau without fish. Today, whenever Ronaldo goes to a restaurant and orders his favorite meal, he always asks for an extra helping of codfish.

"I Had No Toys"

Cristiano's house stood at the top of a long narrow road named Rua Quinta Falcão. The road was very steep. Like most boys in the neighborhood, Cristiano loved playing *futebol* (known as soccer in the United States). Because it was a very poor area, Santo António had no public

13

parks, playgrounds, or town soccer fields for children to play organized games. Instead, Cristiano and his friends played on the street, pretending to be members of Real Madrid, the Spanish team that is considered to be the greatest European soccer club of all time. They set up trashcans to mark the goals. The boys learned quickly to keep control of the ball; those who couldn't were always chasing balls down the hill. Cristiano and his friends also had to watch out for traffic. "Whenever a bus came along, it had to stop a little while [and] wait for us to take the goals out of the way," he recalled.[4]

Growing up poor, Cristiano had few, if any, belongings. Soccer meant everything to him. Without a soccer ball of his own, he wadded up his socks to form a ball. He dribbled the sockball, first with his right foot, then with his left, around an obstacle course of furniture inside the cramped little house. He did this over and over again, even with his eyes closed. He practiced until it was perfect every time. Cristiano knew the moves. By the time he was six years old, attending Andorinha soccer matches with his father had become a regular activity. After watching a match, Cristiano came home and with his sockball quickly mastered the moves he had witnessed.

> I was brought up with nothing. I had no toys and no Christmas presents.[5]

Cristiano desperately wanted a soccer ball of his own. Through his father's work as an equipment manager for CF Andorinha, he received a cherished gift. One day, his father brought home a used, beat-up soccer ball. He played constantly with his second-hand ball; it became his most prized possession.

"He slept with his ball, it never left his side," said his godfather, Fernão Sousa. "It was always under his arm; wherever he went, it went with him."[6]

Lombinho Street

Soccer's importance was gradually growing stronger in Cristiano's life. Even when friends did not join him in a game of soccer, he found ways to practice by himself. Cristiano had a favorite wall just up the street from his house that was ideal for practicing his kicks. He kicked

Where in the World Is Madeira?

Madeira is a mountainous island of volcanic rock located 500 miles (805 kilometers) southwest of Lisbon, Portugal, and 400 miles (644 km) west of Morocco, Africa, in the North Atlantic Ocean. The island is a popular vacation spot, famous for its Madeira wine, near-perfect climate, beautiful beaches, and luxurious hotels enjoyed by tourists year-round.

The capital city of Madeira is Funchal. It is located on the southern side of the island and has a population of around one hundred thousand people. The name of the city is derived from the abundance of the fennel herb, called *funcho* in Portuguese. Funchal is known for its lavish flower gardens and its spectacular annual New Year's Eve fireworks show.

the ball against the cement wall with his right foot, caught it with his left heel, skillfully rolled it back over to his right instep, and kicked the ball again. Because the ball rebounded so quickly off the wall, it sharpened his reflexes. He also learned to retrieve and control the ball, just as he would have to do against an opponent in a real game.

Each day after school Cristiano waited for the older neighborhood boys to walk past his house. He knew they were going to play soccer. The older boys liked to play on Lombinho Street, where it was flat. He watched out the window for the usual group of boys to pass by on their way to play their own pickup game. Cristiano grabbed his ball and scampered outside. He scurried up the hill, quickly touching the ball back and forth between his right foot and his left foot. Cristiano, at seven, had already learned to control the ball with either foot, which is a skill that many players his age were not yet comfortable doing. When he pulled alongside the other boys, he balanced the ball smoothly on the laces of his right shoe and then delicately flicked it back up into the air, where he caught it on his head. The older boys laughed and took notice of the kid's ability and showmanship.

One day, the older boys were one player short of even sides, so Cristiano was invited to play along. He was stunned. Every boy on the team was twelve years old. All of them were far bigger and stronger than he was. Cristiano's heart was virtually trembling with excitement. The older boys were tough, but he was tough, too. Cristiano so impressed the older boys with his quickness and dribbling ability that day that they would often invite him to play along with them. This concerned his mother. She was worried that her son might get hurt. "My husband was always encouraging him to play with older kids," she said. "I was worried he could hurt himself or break a leg, but Dinis always said, 'Don't worry, they can't catch him, he's too fast.'"[7]

Finding Direction

· ·

From an early age, Cristiano Ronaldo adored playing soccer. He was almost never without a ball. He also watched the game constantly, studying how other players dribbled and passed and all the angles they used to create space. Although the Aviero family couldn't afford a television of their own, Cristiano was often invited over to a friend's house to watch a match. Afterward, he came home and with his sockball worked hard to copy the moves he saw. His talent, enthusiasm, and passion for the game soon became apparent. He was a kid who ate, drank, and slept the game. Football was everything to him.

One day, while watching a program about World Cup soccer, he was amazed to see how Johan Cruyff, the legendary Dutch player, faked a defender out of his cleats. He wanted to master that move, so he practiced for hours indoors with his sockball. Doing his best to copy Cruyff's movements, Cristiano raised his right leg

Dutch soccer star Johan Cruyff influenced a young and impression-
able Cristiano Ronaldo. Cruyff executed a feint that subsequently
was named the Cruyff Turn and was soon copied the world over.

as if he was going to fake a pass and then flicked the ball behind his left leg in a quick change of direction. Then he alternated feet, first using his right foot to move left, then his left foot to move right. He did this hundreds of times until it was perfect. He even did it with his eyes closed. All that practice paid off.

Natural Talent

Cristiano joined Clube de Futebol Andorinha de Santo António (abbreviated as CF Andorinha), the soccer club where his father worked. At eight, he was one of the smallest boys on the field, but he quickly showed signs of being a fierce competitor. In his first game wearing the blue and white Andorinha jersey, as soon as the ball was in play, Cristiano bolted forward and took hold of it.

Johan Cruyff

In the early 1970s, Dutch soccer star Johan Cruyff (1947–2016) was a three-time winner of the Ballon d'Or as the world's best player of the year. He led the Netherlands to the 1974 World Cup final and received the Golden Ball as the tournament's most outstanding player. During the tournament he executed a feint that subsequently was named the Cruyff Turn and was soon copied the world over. He led Ajax to three consecutive European Cup (now known as Champions League) victories from 1971 to 1973 before moving to Barcelona for a then world record transfer fee. He also led Ajax and Barcelona to multiple titles as manager of both clubs.

This fearless, take-charge style of play impressed his new coach, Francisco Afonso.

"He was something special from the start, you could see that," said the coach. "He was small but so determined. He started as a defender but soon moved up the pitch because he wanted to be involved in everything. He always wanted the ball."[1]

With the ball seemingly glued to his feet, Cristiano was fast as lightning, faster than any other boy. When he took hold of the ball, he dribbled downfield, driving the ball forward with each racing stride. He left defenders in his dust, unable to catch up. Staring down the goalkeeper, he nudged the ball forward with his left foot, swung back his right foot, and struck the ball hard and low to the far post, with perfect form. The ball rocketed into the corner of the net for an easy score. Everyone else on the field looked helpless as Cristiano celebrated his first goal for Andorinha.

He was just getting started. Minutes later, as a defender closed in, he instinctively used his newly perfected move. Closely controlling the ball and maneuvering to the right, with his back to the defender, Cristiano executed the Cruyff Turn. He raised his right foot, dummying a pass, and then deftly tapped the ball behind his left leg, instantly changing direction. He took two more quick dribbles, roared past the defender, and scored again. Cristiano's teammates couldn't believe their eyes. His quick feet and his skill at dribbling the ball were far advanced for a player of his age.

"He was fast, he was technically brilliant and he played equally well with his left and right foot," said

Coach Afonso. "He was skinny but he was a head taller than other kids his age. He was undoubtedly extremely gifted."[2]

Later in the game, when an opponent tried to tackle him, Cristiano was ready with the step-over, an attacking move used to escape a defender. It fools an opponent into thinking you're making a pass when in fact you don't. This is another classic soccer maneuver that Cristiano practiced over and over until he was proficient with both feet. In a flash, he circled over the ball with his right foot and without stopping he did the same with his left foot. Then he finished off the shifty move by tapping the ball in the opposite direction away from the defender, with the outside of his left foot, leaving the opponent dumbfounded.

Because no one could catch Cristiano as he zigged and zagged across the field, his teammates called him Abelhinha, or Little Bee. He was proud of that nickname, and years later when he was living in Madrid he bought a Yorkshire terrier dog that he named Abelhinha.

Schoolboy Star

Soccer was making an impact on Cristiano's life. He was all consumed by it, and the more he played the game, the better he developed his skills. "Some day I'll play for Real Madrid," he told anyone who would listen. Soon his obsession with soccer began to interfere with school. Cristiano quickly discovered that he could not abide by the rules and regulations he was forced to follow at school. He was far more interested in playing soccer than he was in learning arithmetic or cursive handwriting.

REGIONAL

ESCOLAS

ÉPOCA

94-95

ASSOCIAÇÃO
DE FUTEBOL
DO FUNCHAL

NOME CRISTIANO RONALDO DOS SANTOS AVEIRO

CLUBE Clube Futebol Andorinha

LICENÇA N.°

17.182

O SECRETÁRIO GERAL

This ID card was given to eight-year-old Cristiano Ronaldo in 1994 upon joining CF Andorinha. Although he was one of the smallest boys on the field, his quick feet and his skill at dribbling the ball were far advanced for a player of his age.

• •

The lure of playing soccer was always too strong to resist. Many days he pretended to go to school, but then he'd sneak away to go play with his soccer ball instead. Truancy became a fairly common routine. "All he wanted to do as a boy was play football," said his godfather, Fernão Sousa. "He loved the game so much he'd miss meals or escape out of his bedroom window with a ball when he was supposed to be doing his homework."[3]

Cristiano was big for his age, and he was growing up fast—too fast. When he did attend school, he was habitually late, disturbing his classmates while he rushed through the door with an ever-present soccer ball in one hand. His fifth-grade teacher often scolded him for being tardy, urging Cristiano to pay attention to his classwork and not have a one-track mind. Another teacher noticed Cristiano's ingenuity when it came to his favorite sport. "If there wasn't a real ball around," she said, "he would make one out of socks. He would always find a way [to play] football in the playground. I don't know how he managed it."[4]

Like his teachers, Cristiano's mother grew frustrated that her son prioritized his favorite pastime over his school responsibilities. She was determined that he would get a good education. So when Cristiano came home from school, she would firmly tell him to march into his room and complete his homework for the next day. "He always told me he didn't have any," she said. "So I would start [cooking dinner] and he would chance his luck. He would climb out the window, grab a yogurt or some fruit, and run away with the ball under his arm. He'd be out playing until 9:30 at night."[5]

Crybaby

Cristiano earned another nickname during his years playing soccer for Andorinha. This nickname was not so nice, and Cristiano hated it. Nearly all the boys at school had a nickname; often it was a comment on an obvious physical characteristic. Nicknames such as Skinny, Kid, Lefty, and Red were common.

"Without football, my life is worth nothing."[6]

As soon as Cristiano arrived at Andorinha, the

older boys teased him for being a sore loser. Andorinha president Rui Santos remembers a particular game from 1993 against one of the best teams on the island of Madeira. At halftime, Andorinha was losing 2–0. "Ronaldo was so distraught that he was sobbing like a child who had his favorite toy confiscated," he said.[7]

However, he channeled his tearful outburst to create a spark that resulted in an incredible comeback. In the second half, he scored three goals, leading the team to a 3–2 victory. Unable to accept defeat, Cristiano single-handedly willed his team to win. "He definitely did not like to lose," said Santos. "He wanted to win every time and when they lost, he cried."[8]

Though it was clear that Cristiano was highly skilled in terms of agility and ball control, he had not yet learned how to handle failure. His single-minded, must-win-at-all-costs attitude made him a strong-willed player, but it also made winning far more important to him than it was to most of his teammates. They called him Crybaby because of his emotional reactions to losing. "He cried and got angry very easily," his mother said, adding that Cristiano became bad-tempered "if a teammate didn't pass him the ball, if he or someone else missed a goal or a pass, or if the team wasn't playing how he wanted."[9]

Talent Scouts

By the time he was ten years old, Cristiano was already recognized as a phenomenon. His talent was attracting the attention of scouts for Madeira's elite professional teams. These scouts are always on the lookout for highly promising young players. Their goal is to sign these young sensations before another team can. In Cristiano's case, scouts from the two best clubs on the island, Marítimo and Nacional da Madeira, were both very interested in him.

Coincidentally, Cristiano's godfather, Fernão Sousa, had left Andorinha and was now coaching one of the younger Nacional teams. He was pleasantly surprised to learn that the team's scouts were raving about his godson and wanted to sign him to a training contract. But he also knew it would not be easy. Marítimo was Cristiano's favorite team. And his parents hoped that he would sign with Marítimo because the team's home field was near to the Aviero home; that would make it possible for his parents to watch all of his matches.

Nacional Namesake

Clube Desportivo Nacional, also known as Nacional da Madeira, plays in the Primeira Liga, Portugal's top-tier division of professional soccer. Founded in 1910, the team currently plays its home games at Estádio da Madeira. The stadium is located in the north of Funchal, high in the mountains of the Choupana district.

In 2007, Nacional opened a youth training facility, Cristiano Ronaldo Campus Futebol, an academy named after the club's most famous player. The campus is comprised of four small fields used in the training of Nacional's youth teams and a mini-stadium that seats eight hundred people.

Little boys with big dreams gather near a portrait of Cristiano Ronaldo, taken when he was an eight-year-old player with CF Andorinha, their local soccer club.

• •

A meeting was scheduled with both teams so Cristiano's parents could make a decision on which was the better choice for their son. However, when the Marítimo representative missed the meeting, Dinis and Dolores decided that their son would sign a contract with Nacional. Without realizing it, the ten-year-old had just made his first step toward a professional career.

From Madeira to Portugal

· · · · · · · · · · · · · · · · · · · ·

Cristiano Ronaldo had just turned ten years old when he arrived at the Nacional da Madeira training facility in Funchal. Many of the best players from the island trained there. For the first time, he would be playing with boys as skilled and talented as he was. It seemed they were all far bigger and stronger, too. The coaches at Nacional noticed how skinny Cristiano was, and they were concerned his slight build might hold him back. They wanted him to eat more to fill out his scrawny frame.

Cristiano eyed the other boys and realized his coaches were right. He decided to bulk up and began eating more at every meal. The cafeteria at the training center offered more food than Cristiano had ever seen in his life, and he ate everything in sight, even his vegetables. Then he went home in the evenings and ate a family dinner. His mother served him two helpings at each meal, instead of just one.

Gradually, Cristiano put on weight. Soon enough he was holding his own against bigger, more mature boys. He exhibited an innate toughness, like a street fighter, and nothing was going to hold him back. "Street football had taught him how to avoid getting hit, sidestep the opponent and face up to kids much bigger than he was," said Nacional coach Antonio Mendoca. "It had also strengthened his character. He was extremely courageous."[1]

Attracting Notice

The Nacional coaches considered Cristiano a singular recruit. He was talented, he could play with both feet, he was incredibly fast, and when he played it was as if the ball was an extension of his body. However, there was one part of his game that needed an upgrade. He had to accept that soccer is a team sport.

Since the beginning, he had always relied on his ability to dribble the ball down the field and to score almost at will. With Andorinha, he was virtually a one-man team. The idea of sharing the ball and trusting one's teammates was a foreign concept. Yet the Nacional coaching staff stressed cooperation on the field. The coaches yelled at him when he took on a defender rather than pass the ball to an open teammate. Coaches had never corrected him before, and certainly not in front of others. This unfamiliar feeling confused him. Nacional was winning games, and Cristiano was the top scorer on the team. He saw no reason to change his style of play. But to his teammates, he was a ball hog. They tolerated his selfish play, but they didn't appreciate it. "[His teammates] put up with it because he used to score so many goals," said Coach Mendoca. "We won all our games nine- or ten-nil."[2]

By his second season with Nacional, in 1996, Cristiano had learned his lessons well. He was still a prolific goal scorer, but now, his pinpoint passing also created scoring opportunities for others. Players gathered around him, and they celebrated a goal together. Cristiano wanted to be a great player, and he wanted to help his teammates play great, too. At eleven, he was named captain of the ten-to-twelve-year-old team. When that squad went on to win the division title for their age group, it was clear to the coaches that Cristiano was a true leader and motivator.

It was not long before his soccer feats began to attract attention from the best teams on the Portuguese mainland. In March 1997, the president of Sporting Lisbon's fan club in Madeira contacted Aurélio Pereira, the Lisbon club's director of youth recruitment. There was, he said, a gifted young soccer wizard in the academy ranks at Nacional. He thought it would be wise if Pereira went to Funchal to watch Cristiano play to see firsthand how talented the boy was.

Sporting Lisbon (often just referred to as Sporting) is located in the capital city of Portugal and is renowned throughout Europe for its talented youth soccer teams. Sporting's academy has a knack for developing world-class players, like the great Portuguese star Luis Figo. Cristiano's mother was a huge fan of Figo and a rabid Sporting supporter. She was happy with the idea of possibly one day seeing her son in the famous green and white uniform.

Cristiano Ronaldo, right, stretches with a Sporting Lisbon teammate prior to a practice session in 2001. Sporting's academy has a knack for developing world-class soccer players and is renowned throughout Europe for its talented youth soccer teams.

● ●

The Tryout

Sporting Lisbon's Aurélio Pereira agreed to come to Funchal to watch Cristiano play. Pereira planned to evaluate Cristiano while Nacional played in a three-day tournament, but he did not even have to watch Cristiano play to know he wanted to sign him. He found his young target alone on the sidelines waiting for the game to begin, bored and impatient, juggling a bottle of water with his feet. Just from watching Cristiano warm up, the wise scout knew enough. Once the game began, Pereira was amazed by Cristiano's masterful ball control and his graceful touch passes. He was also astonished by the

31

Luis Figo

Luis Figo (b. 1972) is a Portuguese soccer icon who began his professional career with Sporting Lisbon in 1984, then made his name in Spain playing for powerhouse teams FC Barcelona and Real Madrid. In 2005, he moved to Inter Milan, where he played until his retirement in 2009.

Known as the Lion King, the playmaking midfielder led Portugal to the semifinals of the European Championships in 2000 and was named winner of the Ballon d'Or as player of the year. The following year, FIFA (Fédération Internationale de Football Association), the sport's international governing body, named him the World Player of the Year.

He played for Portugal in the World Cups of 2002 and 2006, winning 127 caps, a national team record later broken by Cristiano Ronaldo.

skinny youngster's competitive spirit. "What impressed me most was his determination," said Pereira. "His strength of character shone through. He was courageous. Mentally speaking, he was indestructible. And he was fearless, unfazed by older players. He had the kind of leadership qualities that only the greatest players have. One of a kind."[3]

Pereira was convinced that Cristiano would be a welcome addition at Sporting and was determined to sign him as soon as possible. Within a week, he struck a deal with Nacional to bring Cristiano to Sporting for approximately $27,000, a hefty sum. Sporting had never paid for a youth player, ever, and this was a lot of money even for a young prodigy. Back home, Cristiano and his family were elated when they got the news that a deal had been reached.

Far from Home

Now twelve years old, Cristiano mentally prepared to move almost 600 miles (965 km) away to Lisbon, to train with Sporting's youth team. He was eager to start a new life dedicated to soccer, but he was a bundle of nerves. The thought of moving to unfamiliar surroundings without his family was a scary proposition. For the first time in his life, Cristiano was going to live far away from home. He had never before set foot outside Madeira, and he had little understanding of the world except how to play soccer. "I had never even been on an airplane before," he said. "My sisters and my mother were crying. I was crying."[4]

Cristiano blinked back tears as he waved good-bye to his family and boarded the plane for Lisbon. Ever since he was a little boy, he had dreamed of one day becoming a professional soccer player for Real Madrid. Nothing would keep him from realizing that dream. When he arrived at the Sporting Lisbon youth training

> "There is no harm in dreaming of becoming the world's best player; it is within my capabilities."[5]

grounds in August 1997, he was alone, and he was afraid. "It was very traumatic to leave my family," he said.[6] He went straight to the dormitories near the Estádio José Alvalade and found his assigned room, which he would share with three other boys.

Sporting Lisbon players followed a regimented schedule. This helped newcomers get accustomed to their surroundings. Each morning there was an exercise session of weight lifting and aerobic training. Then the boys attended a nearby school from ten o'clock to five o'clock. After school was another hour of practice.

At Sporting, school was as important as playing soccer. The boys were strongly encouraged to take their studies seriously, for an education would prepare them for a life after soccer. Cristiano Ronaldo's roommates called him Ronnie, and the name stuck. He got along with his roommates, but he was having trouble making

"I Felt Like a Clown"

In August 1997, Cristiano was a newly arrived student at Sporting Lisbon's academy. On the first day of school, he was late finding his way to his new classroom. When he barged in the teacher was already taking attendance. One by one, the students introduced themselves. When it was his turn, Cristiano said his name and then heard some students laughing at him.

"No one understood what I said," Cristiano recalled. "There were times when I thought I spoke a different language [and] I found that very confusing. As soon as I opened my mouth, they immediately started laughing and mocking. I was traumatized. I felt like a clown. I cried with shame."[7]

new friends at school. Classmates mocked him because of his thick Madeira accent. "Nobody could understand me because of my accent," he said. "It was awful."[8]

Living in the big city of Lisbon proved a difficult adjustment, as well. He was homesick and on many nights cried himself to sleep. The Sporting coaches were aware of Cristiano's anxiety. He was not the first island boy who had experienced difficulty adjusting to life at the academy. "I saw that players who came from Madeira, at 15 or 16, had their bag packed again on the second day and were ready to leave, because they missed their family so much," said Aurélio Pereira. "If he wasn't so strong and so convinced that his dream was to become a footballer, he would have quit."[9]

Like the other boys that had come to Sporting from a long distance away, Cristiano was given a prepaid telephone card so he could call home when he needed to speak to his family. He would phone his mother and beg to come home. "I called my mother saying that I could not stand it anymore, that the other kids were making fun of me, that I wanted to return home," he recalled. "'Do not pay attention to what the others say,' my mother and the rest of the family would say. They always gave me the will to continue. I did not give up, thanks to them."[10]

Feeling the Heat

Sporting demanded its players follow a code of conduct and treat teachers, coaches, and teammates with respect. Break the rules and you faced the consequences. Cristiano learned the hard way. He was expelled for threatening a teacher with a chair because he thought

Despite his rocky start, Cristiano Ronaldo eventually began to blossom. Here, the young player, center, displays his masterful ball control skills while playing for Sporting Lisbon in 2002.

• •

the teacher disrespected him. He was also reported for stealing a can of iced tea from a student and two yogurts from a teacher. He also ate the lunches of unsuspecting boys without permission.[11] The worst episode occurred when Cristiano talked back to a coach who asked him to help clean up the locker room. He refused to help, telling the coach, "I'm a Sporting player, and I don't have to pick up anything off the floor."[12]

Not surprisingly, this situation didn't sit well with the team's directors. They decided to punish him in a way that would teach a valuable and lasting lesson. He was told to sit out the next game, a play-off game in Marítimo. Cristiano had been excited to go home to Madeira to play in front of family and friends. When the roster was posted listing the players who would travel to Madeira, his name was missing. "I saw the list and I wasn't on it," he said. "I checked it four times and…nothing."[13]

In a panic, he ran to the training center office to see Aurélio Pereira. "I started crying and stormed into the training center, angrily demanding an explanation."[14] There must have been some mistake, he said. Wasn't he the best player on the team? Yes, Pereira told him. But you were disrespectful to your teacher. You were disrespectful to your coach. That's why we cut you. That's why you won't play.

All of his dreams of going home and playing against Marítimo vanished. Cristiano was devastated. Townspeople would wonder why he wasn't with the Sporting team. He was embarrassed and ashamed. He considered leaving the academy, but cooler heads prevailed.

A Fresh Start

·······················

The team's directors worried that Cristiano might quit and go home. Knowing his mother had a great deal of influence on him, they quickly made arrangements to fly her to Lisbon to stay with her son for a while. The visit lifted Cristiano's spirits considerably.

Heart Scare

When Cristiano was fifteen years old, he began to notice that his heart occasionally seemed to be beating faster than normal. Lying on his bunk or sitting down, for no apparent reason, his heart sometimes raced. Troubled, he admitted to a Sporting coach that he sporadically got tired very easily. Team doctors performed a physical examination, monitored his pulse, and detected an irregular heart rhythm. A cardiologist advised surgery to correct the heart defect. "Before we knew exactly what he had, I was worried," said his mother. "There was the possibility of him giving up playing football."[1]

Cristiano was taken to a hospital in Lisbon for an operation. His mother traveled back to the mainland to nurture and support him. It wasn't immediately known if he would ever play competitive soccer again. His professional career was in jeopardy before it ever began.

Training Days

Thankfully, the heart ailment was less serious than the doctors had feared. Cristiano was sidelined only a few weeks and made a full recovery. He returned to training with renewed commitment.

At Sporting, players trained for hours each day. Cristiano wanted to do more to improve his strength and endurance. There was a weight room in a gym next to the dormitory. On many nights, he would jump over a wall and sneak into the gym, usually without permission. He spent many solitary hours lifting weights and training to get stronger. To improve his quickness,

Smooth Operation

Doctors used a laser to fix a part of Cristiano's heart that was causing it to beat so fast. The procedure, called a catheter ablation, selectively destroys areas of the heart that are causing a heart rhythm problem. Thin, flexible wires called catheters are inserted into a vein, typically in the upper leg. The wires are threaded up through the vein and into the heart. There is an electrode at the tip of each wire. The electrode emits radio waves that create heat. This heat destroys the heart tissue that causes the fast heart rate.

he ran long distances with heavy sandbags tied to his legs. The extra weight forced his lower body to work harder and, as a result, strengthened his thigh and calf muscles. The extra-strong legs, defenders discovered, made Cristiano and the ball nearly inseparable. He even raced automobiles on the street. "Ronaldo would go and wait by the stop sign," Aurélio Pereira recalled. "There is a ramp immediately after it. Ronaldo would tie weights to his legs, and wait for the light to turn green. Then he would race the cars up the ramp."[2]

Hard work was paying off, as Cristiano continued moving up the ranks of Sporting Lisbon. His frequent promotions to better teams, with older players, made him a mini-celebrity on the academy campus grounds. While some kids used to tease him about his accent, no one was teasing him about his soccer skills. Other boys had once made fun of him as a sore loser or had laughed at him because of the funny way he spoke. Now those same boys admired and respected him.

Moving Up

The laser surgery on Cristiano's heart turned out to be a blessing. He felt a significant improvement in his endurance. In the first game after his surgery, the coaching staff scrutinized his every move when he took the field. They sat in awe as he charged down the field faster than any of the older boys. It was as if he doubled his speed, and he never seemed to run out of energy. It was a medical miracle, thought Sporting manager Augusto Inácio.

A health scare might have inspired Cristiano to work harder and dedicate himself even more deeply to soccer. His hard work paid off.

The manager started the fifteen-year-old Cristiano on the under-sixteen team. Within two weeks, after showing off his incredible individual artistry on the field, he was advanced to the under-seventeen team. Inácio put him and the under-seventeens up against the under-eighteen squad, and Cristiano's side won. The next day, he moved up again. At fifteen, he became the first player in Sporting's history to go from the under-sixteen team all the way to the under-eighteen team in the same season.

Tipping Point

Already known for his unmatched skill at getting the ball to heel, sit, and roll over like a trained Labrador, Cristiano was also improving his field vision and positioning. He displayed a canny ability to predict the outcome of a play in progress and to be in the right spot at the right time when the ball arrived at his feet. Soccer intelligence was putting him in situations to show off his extremely powerful kick. His goal-scoring output increased exponentially, and he was developing into one of the best finishers at Sporting Lisbon.

In August 2001, Sporting offered Cristiano a professional contract. It was a four-year deal worth about $2,000 a month. He signed it, and after cashing the first paycheck, he sent the money home to pay for his brother's drug rehabilitation program.

His father had checked into rehab, too, for his drinking. José Dinis Aveiro battled alcoholism most of his adult life. Heartbroken, Cristiano prayed for his father's treatment to work. His father had always been his most vocal supporter, attending every game he could, and cheering enthusiastically from the sidelines. Long before Cristiano became famous, his father bragged to friends about Cristiano's accomplishments on the pitch. "My son will be the best player in the world," he would tell them.[3]

Now a professional soccer player with Sporting and earning more money in a month than his family could imagine, Cristiano hired an agent, Jorge Mendes, to guide the next phase of his career. Everything in his life now changed at a rapid pace. He moved out of the dorm room and into his own apartment in Lisbon, and he quit school. Though his parents would have preferred he stay in school, realistically, they knew he had no interest in academics. He had always neglected his studies. "I am sorry I did not study more," he says today, "but I had to make a choice in my life."[4]

The Sporting directors urged Cristiano to stay in school, but Dinis and Dolores did not force him to. Like all parents, they wanted their child to have a better life than they had. Cristiano's opportunity for wealth and fame, they thought, might likely come from playing soccer. He was a star in Portugal, but to be an international star he needed to train and practice as much as possible.

Coming of Age

Cristiano was sixteen when he reported for permanent duty with Sporting's first team. Now he would be training regularly with players who were eighteen to twenty-two years old. Though he was shrewd and shifty, due to his youth, the coaches limited his playing time to about twenty minutes a game. His big breakthrough occurred in a game against Real Betis, from Spain, in the fall of 2002. He entered as a substitute with only thirteen minutes left to play and the score tied. The game went into overtime, meaning the next goal for either team

A Homecoming

Cristiano Ronaldo was welcomed like a king when he returned to Portugal's Estádio José Alvalade and took the field for Real Madrid, against Sporting Lisbon, in a Champions League match in November 2016. The Portuguese star picked up an assist on a first-half goal to spark the 2–1 victory for Real Madrid.

The game was a homecoming of sorts for Ronaldo, who started his career at Sporting. Portuguese fans left little doubt as to just how much he means to them. His name was loudly cheered during the announcement of the Real team, and a banner was unfurled by the home fans with the message "Made in Sporting" with a picture of a teenage Ronaldo wearing their famous green and white jersey.

More than twenty years have passed since he said good-bye to Sporting Lisbon, but Ronaldo's first professional team remains tremendously proud of all that its most prized alumnus has accomplished. His image has been emblazoned on a mural outside the dressing rooms of Sporting's Estádio José Alvalade. At Sporting's youth academy in Alcochete, the walls are adorned with pictures of Ronaldo, and two autographed jerseys from his Manchester United days hang behind the director's desk.

Ronaldo, right, trained with members of Portugal's national team in 2002. Many of the top clubs in England, Spain, and Italy, were paying close attention to the exciting teenager from Portugal and dispatched their best recruiters to watch him play.

• •

would win the match. Cristiano stole the ball, and from an impossible angle, scored the game-winning goal. Triumphant, he ran around the field in celebration, blowing kisses to fans in the stands, announcing he had arrived.

Due to his outsized athletic gifts, Cristiano always played soccer with boys several years older. He was eight when he played with the twelve-year-olds on Lombinho Street, and twelve when he played with the sixteen-year-olds for Nacional da Madeira. By 2003, he was eighteen and playing for Sporting at an under-twenty-one tournament in Toulon, France. Many of the top clubs in England, Spain, and Italy, were paying close attention to the exciting teenager from Portugal and dispatched their best recruiters to France. Cristiano very easily could have been

> I am excited the big clubs have noticed me. It gives me strength to improve every day. [5]

overwhelmed by all the attention he received from clubs eager to sign him. "I don't feel pressured by it at all," he insisted.[6]

Cristiano led his Sporting team onto the victory platform at the under-twenty-one tourney. He raised the championship trophy and solidified his place among the most closely watched soccer players in all of Europe. A horde of screaming fans turned out at the Lisbon airport to welcome home the victors. They were disappointed that Cristiano was not among them. He had stayed back in France, meeting with one of the teams that most wanted to sign the young Portuguese marvel. Cristiano Ronaldo had played his final game for Sporting Lisbon, and it was a triumphant victory. The soccer world was abuzz wondering which team he would play for next.

Playing for a Living

···

Cristiano Ronaldo had journeyed a long way from the streets of Funchal to reach his current destination. Only two years after he had quit school, and only months after his debut with Sporting Lisbon's elite team in the Portuguese league, he agreed to play for Manchester United, one of Europe's most popular and successful professional teams.

The plan was for Ronaldo to remain at Sporting for another year for seasoning, and when he was deemed ready to be called up to play with Manchester, he would sign a contract. The deal would be made public after the upcoming friendly between Sporting Lisbon and Manchester United. It was an exclusive happening because Sporting had just completed construction on its new home grounds, Estádio José Alvalade, and Manchester was on hand for the inaugural contest. The opening of a new soccer stadium would be a historic occasion for the Portuguese soccer community. The stadium would be packed to capacity. Among the screaming fanatics in the grandstand would be a group of interested scouts. Cristiano Ronaldo knew they were all coming to watch him.

Game Changer

More than fifty thousand fans jammed into Estádio José Alvalade. It was a few minutes to game time. Ronaldo's heart pounded. He was eager to play well. He spotted his parents seated in the owner's box. Dinis had finished rehab and stopped drinking, but he did not feel well. The doctors said his kidneys and his liver were in bad shape. Dolores wanted him to see a doctor right away. Dinis agreed to make an appointment, but after the game.

The coach of Manchester United, Sir Alex Ferguson, was also eagerly anticipating the game. Carlos Queiroz, who was a Sporting coach in the 1990s, was now Ferguson's assistant coach at Manchester United. He had been following Ronaldo's progress for the last few years and updating his boss with glowing reports. The teenager from Madeira intrigued Ferguson. The coach heard heroic tales of Ronaldo's goal-scoring adventures, but this was going to be his first chance to get a good look at the kid in a big game.

The match started slowly. At the fifteen-minute mark, Ronaldo finally broke through. He fired a shot at Fabien Barthez, the Manchester United goalkeeper, but the Frenchman sent the ball careening over the crossbar. That was the story of the game for Ronaldo. He turned the defenders marking him inside out, creating several scoring chances on his own, but he couldn't finish. He did everything but put the ball in the net.

Ferguson sat on the visitor's bench and never took his eyes off Ronaldo. The Man U coach loved his technical skills, his hustle, and his powerful shots on

Manchester United coach Sir Alex Ferguson, considered by many to be the greatest soccer coach of all time, welcomes Cristiano Ronaldo to the storied English club after Ronaldo signed a historic contract to play for the Red Devils, in 2003.

goal. At one point, Ronaldo threaded a pinpoint pass to a teammate who in turn scored the first Sporting goal. An inspired Sporting club was propelled to a surprising 3–1 upset win. Playing near perfect in what he called "the most important [game] of my life,"[1] Ronaldo showed everything in his talented bag of tricks. The kid even wowed the spectators with a crowd-pleasing bicycle kick.

When the match was over, Ferguson told his Portuguese assistant that he did not want to leave Lisbon without Ronaldo. The coach admitted that the eighteen-year-old was "one of the most exciting young players I've ever seen."[2] Queiroz relayed the message to Ronaldo's agent and said that his client should travel with Man U back to England. Ferguson said: "After we played

Manchester United

Manchester United is a professional soccer team based in Manchester, England. Nicknamed the Red Devils for their distinctive red jerseys, the club was founded in 1878 and today is one of the most popular and successful sports team in the world.

Man U has won the top-division Premier League title a record twenty times and the Football Association Cup twelve times. In 1968, the squad became the first English club to win the European Cup, with a 4–1 victory over Benfica of Portugal in the final. In the 1998–1999 season, Man U secured the first treble in English football history by winning the Premier League, the Football Association Challenge Cup (known as the FA Cup), and the Champions League.

Sporting, the lads in the dressing room talked about him constantly, and on the plane back from the game they urged me to sign him. That's how highly they rated him."[3]

First Impressions

Ronaldo traveled to England to sign a five-year contract with one of the most distinguished football clubs on the European continent. Manchester United paid handsomely for him. Sporting agreed to sell Ronaldo to Man U for a transfer fee of about $15 million—one of the highest fees paid for such a young player in the history of the sport. Then there was the matter of his salary. At Sporting, he had received a monthly stipend of about $2,000, with much of it going back to his parents in Madeira. At Man U he was earning about $150,000 per month, an astronomical raise!

As word got out about the acquisition of the teenager from Portugal, many Red Devil fans were not sold on the deal. They wondered whether such a young, virtually untested player could be worth that much money. One British newspaper reporter pointed out that Ronaldo, with only twenty-five first-team appearances on Sporting Lisbon, had become "the most expensive teenager in the history of the British game."[4]

Skeptical fans grew even more concerned about the wisdom of signing the youngster when a tabloid newspaper published photographs of him crossing a Manchester street with his mother holding his hand. Immature mama's boy, the critics jeered. Older fans, concerned about the I'm-too-cool-for-school attitude, questioned his earnestness when he showed up at the introductory press conference wearing a T-shirt and faded blue jeans, his hair streaked with highlights, and a sly smirk from underneath his backward baseball cap. Soon enough, however, Ronaldo's enchanting personality charmed them all, even the most outspoken naysayers. "I am very happy to be signing for the best team in the world," he said, "and especially proud to be the first Portuguese player to join United."[5]

British Invasion

Just as the young Ronaldo had benefited by developing his game at the Sporting youth academy, he now had the chance to continue to progress as a soccer player under the support of Sir Alex Ferguson. A former player, Ferguson managed Manchester United from 1986 until 2013, winning thirteen English Premier League titles and numerous other trophies. He is considered by many to be the greatest soccer coach of all time.

Ferguson told Ronaldo to stay in England and begin training immediately. Shocked, Ronaldo told him that all of his things were back in Lisbon and that he had not yet said good-bye to his family. Ferguson reassured him that he would train in England but he could return to Portugal soon to get his belongings. Ferguson also went to great lengths to reassure Ronaldo's mother, who was concerned about her son going to live so far away. She said that Ferguson promised that

"[Sir Alex Ferguson] was a football father to me."[6]

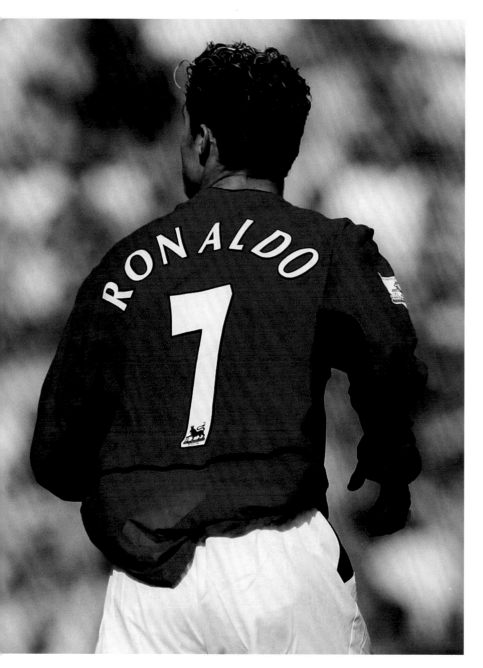

Upon joining Manchester United, Ronaldo was assigned the famous number 7 jersey—the same number previously worn by other United greats such as George Best, Eric Cantona, and David Beckham.

he would be sure to keep an eye on Ronaldo in England, since he had no family there. "Ferguson is an exceptional person," she said. "My son has a second father in Manchester who looks after him."[7]

Upon arriving in Manchester, Sir Alex insisted on giving Ronaldo the famous number 7 jersey—the same number previously worn by other United greats such as George Best, Eric Cantona, and David Beckham. Ronaldo was floored. Despite his youth and inexperience, Ferguson had no doubt about Ronaldo's greatness.

Initially, some Manchester United fans believed that it was premature to assign that special number to a teenage rookie. But Ronaldo embraced the honor and responsibility to follow in the footsteps of legends, and CR7 was born. "There's something that the Brits don't know," he said. "Number seven is also special to me because it's the number that Luis Figo wore at Sporting. I have wanted to be like him since I was a little kid."[8]

Rookie Sensation

Ronaldo suited up for his first game in the controversial number 7 jersey when Man U hosted the Bolton Wanderers in the season opener at the venerable Old Trafford stadium, on August 16, 2003. Nicknamed "the Theater of Dreams," Old Trafford has been United's home turf since 1910. With a capacity of over seventy-five thousand, it is the largest soccer stadium in the United Kingdom. For sixty minutes (games are ninety minutes long), the fans screamed for Ronaldo, but he remained seated on the bench, watching his team struggle to hold a 1–0 lead.

Language Barrier

Following his introductory press conference at the Manchester United headquarters, Ronaldo was introduced to one of his new teammates, the great Dutch player Ruud van Nistelrooy. The Dutchman greeted Ronaldo warmly, speaking in English, but Ronaldo had no idea what van Nistelrooy was telling him.

Suddenly, he regretted spending so little time on his studies back in Madeira, especially in English class. "I stood there, looking at him without knowing what to answer, as I could not understand a word he was saying. Then I remembered all the English classes I had skipped. I needed English after all."[9]

In the 61st minute, Ferguson called on Ronaldo to substitute for Nicky Butt. The public address system announced his name, and the crowd roared with delight. He entered the game to a standing ovation. It was time to see what the world's most expensive teenager was made of. Bolton players used intimidation tactics to try knocking Ronaldo off his game, but where he came from, the streets of Funchal, getting beat up was par for the course.

Despite the physicality, he enthralled everyone in the stadium with dazzling dribbles and long circuitous runs from end to end along the wing. He notched an assist on the second goal en route to the Red Devils' 4–0 win and played so well that when he left the field, the Old

In his Manchester United debut, Ronaldo jumps over a tackle during second half action in 2003. Ronaldo entered the game as a substitute and propelled Manchester United to a 4-0 victory. His teammates honored him as the player of the match.

Trafford crowd was on its feet because of the excitement he brought to the game.

"It looks like the fans have a new hero," Ferguson said.[10]

Teammates honored Ronaldo as player of the match and back in the dressing room presented him with a bottle of Champagne as a trophy. "It was a marvelous debut, almost unbelievable," Ferguson said.[11]

The sparkling performance also earned praise from George Best, who hailed it as "undoubtedly the most exciting debut" he had ever seen.[12]

The Changing World

....

A whole new reality was awaiting Cristiano Ronaldo in England, a new country, with a new way of thinking about soccer. Ronaldo scored six goals in his first season in England, including the opening tally in the FA Cup final, helping Manchester United capture that trophy for the first time in four years. The FA Cup is an annual knockout tournament to determine the champion of English football. First played in 1871, it is the oldest soccer competition in the world. Life was smiling on Cristiano Ronaldo. He had won his first team trophy in his first season with MU. The future was looking bright, and the young Portuguese footballer was beaming with confidence.

Call of Duty

The Portuguese national team was in Russia preparing for the 2006 World Cup when Ronaldo received heart-wrenching news. His father, Dinis, had passed away in a

London clinic at the age of fifty-two. Ronaldo had tried hard to help his father overcome alcohol addiction, but in the end, he could not. His father had become extremely ill. Alcoholism had damaged his kidneys and his liver so severely that those organs no longer functioned.

The game against Russia was crucial in Portugal's quest to qualify for the World Cup tournament. Still, the Portugal coaches recommended the twenty-year-old return to his family and take the time he needed to grieve over his father's death. Ronaldo refused, telling his coaches that he wanted to play in the game the next day as a way to honor his father. "My dad would want me to play," he explained. "He always did everything in life for me to play football."[1]

Ronaldo hoped to score a goal against Russia to dedicate to his father. Though the game finished in a scoreless tie, he still played a starring role and helped his country secure the vital point it needed to qualify for the upcoming World Cup.

The Winking Incident

The fiercely competitive World Cup tournament in 2006 came at great personal cost for Ronaldo, and there would be a professional cost, too. Ronaldo clashed with Wayne Rooney, his teammate at Manchester United, who was playing for his home country of England. In the quarterfinal match pitting Portugal against England, the two players were involved in an incident that caused a bitter rift between the loyal fans of both countries.

The friction began when Rooney was whistled for a foul after stomping on a Portuguese defender with his

Cristiano Ronaldo arrives at his father's funeral at the Santo António cemetery in Funchal in 2005. His father, Dinis, who battled an alcohol addiction for most of his adult life, had passed away a few days earlier in a London clinic at the age of fifty-two.

cleats. Ronaldo complained aggressively to the referee that Rooney's action was a cheap shot and that he should receive a red card (meaning that he would have to leave the field and could not be substituted for, leaving England a man short). The referee, after much thought, did eventually issue Rooney a red card, and after Rooney was sent off, Ronaldo was seen winking to Portugal's bench. Many believed he had unfairly influenced the referee to get his club teammate sent off and then cracked wise to his national teammates with a sarcastic gesture.

England now had to play one man short for nearly an hour. They battled on bravely for the rest of regulation time and extra time, taking the game to a shoot-out. Ronaldo scored the winning goal of the shoot-out and exploded in celebration with an emotional show of public tribute to his father. With millions watching around the world he pointed to the sky and burst out yelling: "This one's for you! "[2]

Portugal won the game against England and reached its first World Cup semifinal match in forty years, only to lose to France as the crowd heavily booed Ronaldo. He insisted he was not to blame for Rooney's dismissal, despite appearing to wink at the Portuguese bench once the red card had been shown. "I am not a referee and I don't have the power to send off a player," he said. "I had nothing to do with the fact that the referee showed the red card."[3]

Marked Man

Ronaldo returned from the World Cup in Germany as a pariah after his perceived role in Rooney's expulsion.

"I Was Gobsmacked"

Though England's Wayne Rooney was issued a red card and ejected from a World Cup game against Portugal in 2006, he insisted he was not angry with Cristiano Ronaldo, who appeared to encourage the referee to send him off. "I bear no ill feeling to Cristiano but am disappointed he chose to get involved," the England captain said. "When the referee produced the red card I was amazed—gobsmacked."[4]

Yet Rooney holds no grudge against Ronaldo. "I understood why he did it. He was trying to win for Portugal. I would probably do the same if it was the other way round."[5]

When the Premier League season resumed, Ronaldo was made the scapegoat for England's elimination from cup competition. Many soccer experts at the time did not see how he could ever go back to England and play for Manchester United after a match in which he was, rightly or wrongly, held responsible for the ejection of his MU teammate, leading to England's crushing defeat.

Many fans now saw Ronaldo as an enemy, and he was vilified as "the most hated man in England."[6] The media stoked the controversy, as well. A British tabloid, the *Sun*, printed a cover picturing Ronaldo's face on a dartboard, with his winking eye on the bull's-eye. "Here's every England fan's chance to get revenge on the world's biggest winker," it read.[7]

Ronaldo was now a target of every British soccer fan's ire. The hatred toward him could be seen and heard in every stadium outside Old Trafford that the Red Devils went to visit. To a chorus of boos, he made his United return in a preseason friendly at Oxford. Appearing totally unfazed by the derision aimed in his direction, he scored two goals in the Man U victory. But the booing and insults made Ronaldo think about leaving England and Manchester United. He did not want to play in a country where fans hated him. It was around this time that he started publicly talking about a move to Real Madrid, which is closer to his native Portugal. "I can't stay in England," he said. "Everyone knows my dream is to play in Spain."[8]

After considerable persuasion from Sir Alex Ferguson, Ronaldo was convinced to stay at Man U. Against all odds, he responded to the public criticism by producing his most productive season yet in the English Premier League, as Ferguson's faith in Ronaldo was rewarded. He scored his fiftieth Manchester United goal against crosstown rival Manchester City, on May 5, 2007, and finished the club season by netting twenty-three goals, helping Manchester United capture the English Premier League title for the first time in four years.

> Scoring goals gives me the happiest feeling in the world. I just love it.[9]

In March 2007, Manchester United had committed over $30 million to Ronaldo as part of a five-year contract extension, and to justify his newly signed contract, he put together one of the club's finest seasons in history, setting a franchise record by scoring forty-two goals and leading Manchester United to the English Premier League title for a second straight year.

Career Crossroads

Ronaldo is perhaps the greatest header of the ball among all the current players. At 6 feet 1 inch and 185 pounds (185.42 cm; 84 kg), with incredibly strong thighs, he relies on a 30-inch (76-cm) vertical leap—a jumping ability that surpasses that of the average professional basketball player—to climb to a remarkable height of 8 feet 7 inches (261.62 cm), rising well above the defenders, to win the ball. And the hang time, to borrow a basketball phrase,

Testing Limits

Ever wonder what it is that sets Cristiano Ronaldo apart from other great athletes? In 2011, leading sports scientists at the University of Chichester, using the latest technology in a high-performance laboratory, put Ronaldo through a series of elaborate challenges that show exactly what gives him the edge to perform at an elite level. The famous Ronaldo free kick was tested to determine if its strength and power were enough to shatter walls of glass. He went head-to-head against an elite sprinter in a contest of speed and agility by running a zigzag course and took part in a unique soccer skills experiment conducted in total darkness. The astonishing results are explained in a one-hour documentary film titled *Ronaldo: Tested to the Limit*.

Ronaldo, who boasts a 30-inch vertical leap that enables his body to float in the air for nearly one second, is perhaps the greatest header of the ball among all the current players.

is 0.7 seconds, enabling his body to float in the air for nearly one second.[10]

Ronaldo scored a memorable goal on a towering header in the Champions League quarterfinal against Sportiva Roma at Rome's Stadio Olimpico, on April 1, 2008. A crossing pass soared in front of the goal, and Ronaldo jumped, his body hanging ever so gracefully in the air for one, two, three beats, seemingly defying gravity. At the apex of his jump, his back was arched. His eyes were forward, locked on the target. Then he snapped his neck like a cobra pursuing its prey. The contact was flawless, and the ball, as if it had engines attached, whizzed past the goalkeeper and rippled the bottom corner of the net. Ronaldo scored with yet another beautiful header in the final match as Man U was crowned champion of Europe for the third time in its illustrious history.

Accepting his first Champions League medal, Ronaldo was named the tournament's most outstanding player. For his stellar performance during the season he earned the Ballon d'Or trophy as the world's best soccer player of the year. It was the first time a Manchester United player had won the trophy since George Best won it in 1968. Predictably, Ronaldo's success led some people to compare him with the former Man U legend, prompting Best to say, "There have been a few players described as 'the new George Best' over the years, but this is the first time it's been a compliment to me."[11]

The following season, Ronaldo scored twenty-six goals as MU collected its third consecutive English Premier League title, a noteworthy team achievement.

Ronaldo scored a crucial goal against Porto in the Champions League quarterfinal on a free kick from 40 yards (36.5 m) out. He is known for his free kicks and for the patented knuckleball-style dip effect he gets when taking them. He is also known for the famous pre-kick stance that brings with it the popping flashbulbs from the cameras around the stadium. Approaching the ball, his hips uncoil like a Slinky springing down stairs, as he perfectly strikes the ball in a whiplash action. Goalkeepers tremble when faced with a Ronaldo free kick, usually a screaming shot that travels upwards of 80 miles per hour (129 kmh), faster than a highway speed limit.

Two more goals by Ronaldo in the semifinal against Arsenal put Manchester United in position to defend its Champions League crown, a feat that hadn't been reached in nearly two decades. Sadly, Man U's quest was an out-and-out failure; they were soundly beaten, 2–0, by Barcelona, with one goal coming from Lionel Messi. It was a disappointing and frustrating way to end the season. For Ronaldo, it was also the end of an era because, as it turned out, he would never again wear the famed red jersey for Manchester United.

Cristiano's Big Move

· · · · · · · · · · · · · · ·

For all his life, Cristiano Ronaldo had been telling people that someday he would love to play with Real Madrid, the famous soccer club based in Spain's capital city. In 2009, speculation swirled that his employment at Manchester United was soon coming to an end. Word leaked that his agent had figured out a way for Ronaldo to move to Real Madrid. Manchester's coach, Sir Alex Ferguson, emphatically denied that a deal had been struck to send his star to the Spanish league, insisting he would never negotiate a contract with "that mob" at Real Madrid, adding, "I wouldn't sell them a virus."[1]

Still, no one was surprised when Ronaldo left Manchester in the summer of 2009 for a six-year contract with Real Madrid. He walked out of Old Trafford having won the Champions League, three Premier League titles, the FA Cup, and the Club World Cup in six seasons with Manchester United. Among the team's most-ever celebrated players, Ronaldo scored 118 goals in 292 appearances, a commendable achievement in one of the world's top leagues.

Real Madrid paid Man U a transfer fee of $131 million, at the time, the most money ever paid for a player in the history of the sport. It was a risky gamble for a team to invest so much on one player. Real Madrid, not wanting to lose their prized investment, also put a $1 billion buyout clause on Ronaldo, making sure he would stay at Madrid for years to come. During his transfer, Ronaldo said, "People understand my decision and respect that. It was my dream to play in Madrid."[2]

Real Deal

Real Madrid was founded in 1902 as Madrid Football Club. The team's name was changed to Real Madrid in 1920, after King Alfonso XIII of Spain granted to the club the title of *real*, which means "royal" in English.

Real Madrid's kingly status is due to club president Santiago Bernabéu Yeste (1895–1978), who constructed a bona fide dream team during the 1950s and 1960s centered on the talents of Alfredo Di Stéfano. Wearing their traditional white uniforms, the Real team that claimed the first five European Cups from 1956 to 1960 is still considered by many to be the greatest football team ever assembled.

With a record thirty-two La Liga titles, nineteen Copa del Rey trophies, and eleven European Cups/Champions League titles, Real is second to none among the greatest football clubs of all time.

"Viva Madrid!"

To welcome Ronaldo to Madrid, the Real club hosted a public introduction of the Portuguese idol at Santiago Bernabéu stadium on July 6, 2009. Fans, many of whom had been dreaming of this day for three years, began lining up outside the stadium in the early morning, hoping to glimpse the twenty-four-year-old winger from Madeira. Inside, more than eighty thousand Real Madrid fans showed up to welcome the world's most expensive footballer. "I am so happy to be here," a beaming Ronaldo said before leading fans in a cry of "*Viva Madrid!*" "I have made my childhood dream a reality."[3]

More than eighty thousand Real Madrid fans showed up to welcome Ronaldo during his public introduction in 2009. The Portuguese star led fans in a cry of "Viva Madrid!" and told the crowd that playing for Real Madrid was his childhood dream come true.

Since Real Madrid captain Raúl already wore the jersey with number 7 on it, Ronaldo received the number 9 shirt that had once been worn by club legends Hugo Sanchez, Ronaldo (of Brazil), and Alfredo Di Stéfano. After performing a few juggling tricks, he completed a lap of honor to salute fans. The ecstatic fans gave Ronaldo a roaring welcome so exuberant the soccer star had to be hustled away by security guards when spectators leaped barriers and took the field. The crowds at Santiago Bernabéu, Madrid's famous stadium, were sure that they had found a star that would bring them back to greatness.

Manning Up

Surprising off-the-field news broke in the summer of 2010. On June 17, Ronaldo, twenty-five, became a father, announcing on his Facebook page the birth of his son, Cristiano Junior. The identity of the baby's mother, thought to be an American woman, has always remained a secret, and Cristiano Junior is under his father's exclusive guardianship.

The news shocked many fans, as did the big mystery concerning who the baby's mother was. The tabloids were abuzz with rumors, but Ronaldo has never revealed the identity of his son's mother, and he swears he never will. The child is in the tender loving care of Ronaldo's mother, Dolores, and his older sisters, Elma and Liliana Cátia.

Cristiano Junior frequently visits stadiums to see his father play. In the Euro 2012 quarterfinal against Holland, won by Portugal, 2–1, Ronaldo scored both goals. After scoring the first goal he sucked his thumb and pointed up to his private box and waved at Cristiano Junior. Said the proud papa, "I'm very happy because today is also my son's birthday and I dedicate both my goals to him."[4]

Fatherhood changed Ronaldo. Caring for another human being is a responsibility that affected him in a way that made him feel more comfortable with the emotions he experienced on the soccer field. Win or lose, the joy of coming home to his child reprioritized Ronaldo's life, and positive or negative soccer results were put into proper perspective. This new outlook translated to even greater success on the pitch.

New Era

A devastating haul of thirty-three goals in thirty-five appearances (despite missing a month and a half with injury) rendered Ronaldo's first season in Spain a huge personal success. Unfortunately, no team trophies were forthcoming, as Barcelona continued its domestic dominance in La Liga (Spanish for "league"), and Real Madrid again bowed out of the Champions League in the second round. In 2010, with the departure of Raúl from Madrid, Ronaldo was given the number 7 jersey, and a new era for CR7 was underway. Ronaldo helped Real Madrid capture the Copa del Rey, scoring the winning goal against Barcelona in the final, to earn his first trophy as a member of Real Madrid. He also bested the all-time scoring record for most goals in a season in the Spanish league, turning on the afterburners (eleven in the final four games) to take his tally to forty.

The arrival of son Cristiano Junior in 2010 changed Ronaldo's life for the better. The identity of his son's mother has always remained a secret.

· ·

In any other year, scoring forty goals would have been enough to win the Ballon d'Or, but despite Ronaldo's outrageous goal-scoring prowess, Lionel Messi of Argentina took home the individual prize. The next year, Ronaldo came back even stronger with his best to date. He netted forty-six goals in the league and sixty in all competition as Real reclaimed the Liga title away from Messi's Barcelona team, much to the delight of Real fans. Ronaldo's goal in a 2–1 victory at Barcelona's Camp Nou stadium all but ensured Real Madrid's first Spanish league title since 2008.

Ronaldo had now scored one hundred goals in just three seasons at Madrid, the fastest player in Spanish league history to reach the century mark. The following season Ronaldo scored fifty-five goals in fifty-five games and was the top scorer of the Champions League with twelve goals. He was averaging nearly a goal per game—a rate of scoring efficiency that borders the unbelievable. It seemed like the only person he was competing against for his goal-scoring records was himself—and Lionel Messi, of course.

Storied Rivalry

Ronaldo's arrival to the Spanish league was also the beginning of his great rivalry with Lionel Messi, the Argentinean soccer star who plays for Barcelona, Real Madrid's chief rival in La Liga. After Ronaldo's first season at Madrid, he finished second in the voting for the Ballon d'Or behind Messi, who would go on to win the award for four straight years, with Ronaldo finishing runner-up in three of those four years. A legion of supporters spoke out in favor of Ronaldo. Madrid's coach at the time, José Mourinho, said, "If Messi is the best on the planet, Ronaldo is the best in the universe. If you are going to give out the Ballon d'Or because a player is the best, give it to Cristiano or Messi. But I ask, if the two are

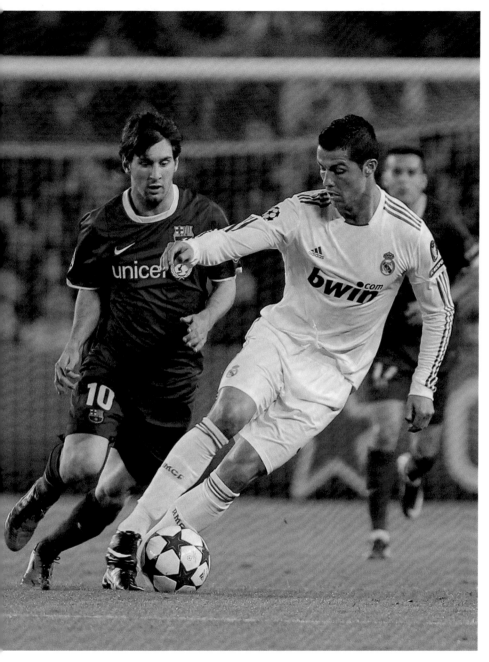

Ronaldo's arrival to the Spanish league was the start of a great rivalry with Argentinean soccer star Lionel Messi, who plays for Barcelona, Real Madrid's chief rival in La Liga.

on the same level, is it normal that one wins four and the other one? It is not."[5]

Ronaldo has since collected his quota of hardware. Messi and Ronaldo have shared the Ballon d'Or prize between them for ten years in a row. El Clásico is one of the most widely watched sporting events in the world, when Messi's Barcelona team plays against Ronaldo's Madrid squad, because of the rivalry. "I'm sure that the competition between us is a motivating factor for him, too," said Ronaldo.[6]

Despite outstanding individual statistics at Real Madrid, Ronaldo is sometimes overshadowed by Barcelona's success and Messi's genius. During Ronaldo's

Presidential Snub

The rivalry between Cristiano Ronaldo and Lionel Messi gained unwanted media attention during a news conference in October 2013. FIFA's president at the time, Sepp Blatter, answered a question about the Ballon d'Or chances for Messi and Ronaldo by praising Messi's quiet and humble demeanor and style of play, while criticizing Ronaldo for being a "commander on the field of play." He also poked fun at Ronaldo's many changing hairstyles, saying, "one of them has more expenses for the hairdresser than the other"[7] before strutting around the stage in apparent mimicry of Ronaldo's unique running style. The president of Real Madrid and the Portugal national team president scolded Blatter for undue influence on Ballon d'Or voters. Blatter later apologized to Ronaldo.

time at Real Madrid he has helped Real win only one Spanish league title, while Messi's Barcelona club has won five. Their rivalry has been a major storyline in the sport, with many people considering Real Madrid and Ronaldo second behind Barcelona and Messi. Ronaldo prefers to play down the personal rivalry. Since he and Messi are two completely different players, he says, it is useless to make comparisons. "You cannot compare a Ferrari with a Porsche," he says.[8]

Drama King

Ronaldo and Messi have distinctly different personalities. While Messi is a closed book, Ronaldo's colorful emotions forever pour out. His often-pained facial expressions indicate disappointment and exasperation in the most obvious ways. He grimaces, frowns, pouts, screams at his teammates, shouts at the referee, and shrieks at the heavens (and at himself) whenever a scoring chance goes awry. To be sure, Ronaldo is not shy; he often removes his shirt while celebrating his goals, showing off a toned torso and chiseled

> "I don't have to show anything to anyone. There is nothing to prove."[9]

abdominal muscles, all while flashing a broad smile capable of lighting up stadium scoreboards as well as photographers' flashbulbs.

What some see as his arrogance on the field is rather an expression of his competitive nature, a self-belief that drives him to achieve new levels of excellence. He wants to win with all his might, and unsurprisingly, this desire many times leads him to push himself and his teammates to be the best they can be. Push sometimes comes to shove. Ronaldo has had some widely reported clashes with teammates, such as a 2006 locker-room brawl with Ruud van Nistelrooy, who accused Ronaldo of showboating.

Never one known for modesty, Ronaldo's conceit may have gone too far, however, in September 2011, when he spoke after a Champions League match against Dinamo Zagreb and responded to the booing of Croatian fans by saying, "I think that because I am rich, handsome, and a great player, people are envious of me."[10]

CHAPTER EIGHT

Portugal's Great Hope

· · · · · · · · · · · · · · · · · ·

Every soccer player dreams of one day winning the World Cup trophy for his or her country. Portugal is a small country, with a population of ten million people—Ronaldo has six times that many Instagram followers—and while Portugal has produced some superior players over the years, it isn't on the same level as Brazil, Argentina, Germany, or Italy, countries that are much bigger and produce many more high-quality players. If Ronaldo were able to win a major international trophy for Portugal, it would be an incredible accomplishment.

Portugal made a great showing at the 2004 European Championships, and Ronaldo scored his first goal for Portugal during that tournament. He converted his penalty kick in a shoot-out against England in the quarterfinal victory and scored the opening goal in a 2–1 win over the Netherlands in the semifinal. Portugal eventually lost to Greece in the final, but the fact that Portugal made it to the European final over traditional powerhouses such as England, Italy, France, and Germany brought a feeling of pride to Ronaldo's home country.

Captain Cristiano

After finishing in fourth place at the 2006 World Cup, Portugal underwent a major overhaul. A new coach, Carlos Queiroz, formerly the assistant at Manchester United, came aboard to steady the ship. By 2008, he named Ronaldo, age twenty-three, as national team captain. Ronaldo captained Portugal to the round of sixteen at the 2010 World Cup, losing 1–0 to eventual champion Spain. Two years later, Spain bested Portugal in the semifinal of the 2012 Champions League in a penalty kick shoot-out. Strangely enough, Ronaldo was set to kick last, but since his other teammates didn't net their penalty kicks and the Spanish side did, Ronaldo never even got a chance to attempt a kick from the spot.

Once again, in agonizing fashion, Spain had dashed its neighbor's dreams of winning a major international competition. Ronaldo promised to persevere. "I will only be content when I have lifted a trophy with Portugal," he said.[1]

For all his success with club teams, Ronaldo faced criticism back in his homeland over his inability to achieve the same for Portugal's national team. Soccer is a team game, of course, and one player can only do so much. Still, many wondered whether he was unable to turn it on against the biggest teams, in the biggest tournaments, when the world was watching. Euro 2004 and 2008 and World Cup 2006 and 2010 yielded little

Ronaldo was failing to translate his success as a club player to the Portuguese national team. Despite his accolaides, he wanted nothing more than to achieve victory for his beloved country.

• •

for Portugal, with unremarkable performances from Ronaldo.

"I Am Here!"

The stakes were high when Portugal traveled to Sweden to play a World Cup qualifying match on November 19, 2013. The winning team would earn a spot in the 2014 tournament, while the loser would have to stay home and wait another four years to try to qualify for the 2018 World Cup.

The fifty thousand spectators at Friends Arena in Stockholm booed when Ronaldo's name was announced during the starting lineups. It was a hostile environment during the action, too; every time Ronaldo received the ball the Swedish crowd taunted him, jeering choruses of "Messi! Messi!"

Playing like a man on a mission, Ronaldo rose to the occasion with a virtuoso performance. He drew first blood five minutes into the second half, giving Portugal a 1–0 lead. After two goals for Sweden, Ronaldo received a pass in stride and sprinted with a defender at his heels before shooting the ball into the net. Having tied the score at 2–2, he celebrated by strutting toward the goal line, staring at the Swedish fans and pointing at himself and then the ground. "I am here!" he screamed.[2]

Two minutes later, flying past defenders on another breakaway, Ronaldo scored again, breaking the hearts of the home crowd. He stunned the fans, and the soccer world, with a magnificent display over twenty-nine minutes of the second half, scoring a hat trick (three goals in one game) to virtually singlehandedly propel Portugal into the World Cup, to be played in Brazil. A reporter with the Portuguese daily sports newspaper *O Jogo* noted there wasn't anything Ronaldo couldn't do for his team: "If it was needed, he'd fly the plane [to Brazil]."[3]

When Portugal landed in Brazil for the 2014 World Cup, Ronaldo was now a bona fide star, hot off of winning his second world player of the year award. Though Portugal made a disappointing early exit in the group stage, Ronaldo scored career goal number fifty for his home country, making him the first Portuguese player to reach that mark in international competition. He also became the first Portuguese footballer to play and score in three World Cup tournaments.

Ego Trips

Anyone with Ronaldo's otherworldly talent—he has made a record 138 national team appearances for Portugal and is the team's top scorer with 79 goals through 2017—would be loved unconditionally and forever considered a native legend. Oddly, that is not always the case with Ronaldo. Despite all he has achieved, he has faced some tough criticism even from Portuguese fans— they have even booed him on occasion. For fans to treat undoubtedly the best player for the nation with such contempt is a remarkable development. Yet Portugal's fans, like most soccer fans, are notoriously hard to please, and over the years, Ronaldo bore the brunt of the Portuguese faithful's frustrations at never having won an international trophy.

Voodoo Curse

A witch doctor from Ghana claimed responsibility for a left knee injury to Cristiano Ronaldo during the 2014 World Cup. The witch doctor, Nana Kwaku Bonsam, whose name translates as Devil of Wednesday, claimed he put a curse on Ronaldo in a bid to help his native Ghana beat Portugal. Even those who don't believe in voodoo were worried when Ronaldo arrived for the Ghana game with an aching knee. The witch doctor claimed to have conjured a special powdery concoction that he sprinkled on a picture of the Real Madrid star to jinx him. The potion didn't work. Ronaldo scored a second-half goal to give Portugal a 2–1 victory.

Perhaps it is his frequent ego trips, his obvious annoyance when teammates flub a scoring chance, and his somewhat selfish style of play that fails to unconditionally endear him to the fans. It has been this way for a long time. Ronaldo has been criticized for his occasional instances of poor sportsmanship, as well. Opponents sometimes complain that he is overly flamboyant. They say he oftentimes takes a dive while trying to draw fouls. Due to his athletic build and his competitive nature, he is often targeted by defenders and endures more than his fair share of hard fouls. "Ronaldo is not protected," said the Portuguese coach José Mourinho. "Rivals see the body of an animal and they kick him."[4]

The showboating step-overs, the playacting dives to draw fouls, the preening, the stomping, the petulance, the narcissism, these are all part of the Ronaldo package. To some, it is too much. To others, it is what makes him appealing. If nothing else, it ensures there are never any doubts as to Ronaldo's feelings during a match.

> "Either you like me or not. There is nothing in between."[5]

Helping Hand

It is easy to forget that Ronaldo has a life outside of soccer and to overlook that he is also a father, a son, and a philanthropist who has devoted his wealth and his fame to help numerous charitable causes around the world.

Still playing at a high level in his early thirties, the combination of Ronaldo's athletic ability and physical fitness will allow him to compete at a high level for many years to come.

In 2013, Ronaldo reunited with an Indonesian boy who survived a massive tsunami that killed more than 230,000 people in December 2004. He maintains his connection to Indonesia by helping preserve mangrove forests, which help buffer against tsunamis.

• • • • • • • • • • • • • • • • • • • •

In December 2004, a devastating earthquake struck beneath the Indian Ocean near Indonesia, generating a massive tsunami, or tidal wave, that killed more than 230,000 people, making it one of the deadliest natural disasters ever recorded. Ronaldo, who was nineteen at the time, visited the area after seeing television coverage that showed a young boy wearing a number 7 Portuguese soccer jersey who was stranded for nearly three weeks after his family was killed. Ronaldo tracked down the boy and helped raise funds for reconstruction of the area. More than a decade later, Ronaldo still maintains his connection to Indonesia and his desire to help its people. He currently is ambassador for the Mangrove Care Forum, an organization in Indonesia aiming to help preserve mangrove forests, which help buffer against tsunamis.

He has even sold some of his valuable trophies for humanitarian causes. In 2011, he won the Golden Boot as Europe's top goal scorer for the season. A year later, he sold the boot for more than $1.5 million and donated all of that money to help build schools for Palestinian children in the war-torn territory of Gaza, which borders Egypt and Israel. In 2012, he paid for a pioneering treatment for a young boy when it seemed that there was no hope left for the child, who had been battling terminal cancer.

He also participates in other altruistic causes. He participates in programs to help children and teenagers

Hometown Hero

Despite being an international star with homes in Spain, New York, and the United Kingdom, Ronaldo still maintains a close relationship with his home of Madeira. In 2010, a major flood affected the people of Madeira. Afterward, he appeared in a charity soccer match to raise funds to help people affected by the flood. Ronaldo also donated money to the hospital in Madeira that saved his mother's life following her battle with cancer so that it could build a new cancer treatment center. Said Ronaldo, "I'm not going to change the world; you're not going to change the world—but we can all help."[6]

around the world avoid drug addiction, HIV, and malaria. In 2013, he began working with Save the Children, helping the fight against child hunger. Recently, he has helped the fight against Ebola, a deadly disease that affects thousands of people, mostly in Africa.

Ronaldo is also one of few modern-day footballers that refrains from being tattooed in the name of fashion. The reason he doesn't have any tattoos is because he donates blood several times during the year to help others, and in some countries, fresh ink can affect how often a person is permitted to give blood.

A player who, despite being a worldwide celebrity, still devotes so much time, energy, and money to help people around the world should hardly be considered arrogant. Yet Ronaldo insists he has gotten more back than he's given away. "My father always taught me that when you help other people, then God will give you double," he said. "And that's what has really happened to me. When I have helped other people who are in need, God has helped me more."[7]

Guts and Glory

· ·

Cristiano Ronaldo made a dream return to Manchester, England, in March 2013, when Real Madrid faced off against his former team in the knockout round of the Champions League. Sir Alex Ferguson, knowing how much the game meant to Ronaldo, arranged for the stadium's public address announcer to introduce the visiting lineup second, leaving Ronaldo's name for last. When Old Trafford was told to "welcome back our magnificent seven, Cristiano Ronaldo,"[1] a rapturous reception echoed around the old yard. The returning hero responded with a wave of his hand and a tap on his heart in return.

Visibly choked up throughout the game, Ronaldo still scored a goal, as Real Madrid won 2–1, to propel the team into the quarterfinal of the European championship. Afterwards, Ronaldo said, "I feel a little bit sad because it is not easy to forget this home. I played for six years here and the people were very nice to me. I came here like a child. It was quite a strange feeling."[2]

In September 2013, Ronaldo signed a new contract that extended his service with Real Madrid for three more years, through 2018. The contract, calling for $22 million per season, made the twenty-eight-year-old the highest paid player in the sport. Real's decision to re-up Ronaldo paid off almost immediately, as he flourished under the tutelage of new coach Carlo Ancelotti, a veteran football manager from Italy, who had taken over the coaching duties from José Mourinho, in the summer of 2013.

At Real Madrid, Ancelotti abandoned the tactics used by his predecessor, switching instead to a 4-3-3 formation to great effect. The scheme proved ideal for Ronaldo and Real Madrid. With a new coach and a new game plan, Ronaldo and his team were positioned to create history and rewrite the record books.

"La Decima"

"La Decima" (meaning "tenth" in Spanish) is the term used for Real Madrid's obsession with winning a tenth European Cup/Champions League title. Real Madrid had not won the Champions League since claiming the trophy for a ninth time in 2002. The team ended its twelve-year quest in the 2014 final against city rival Atlético Madrid, the first time a final had been contested between teams from the same city. Real Madrid won the match 4–1 after extra time, with Ronaldo drilling a goal from the penalty spot to clinch the victory and thus become the first player to score in two Champions League finals for two different winning teams.

This was Ronaldo's second Champions League trophy, but his first for Real Madrid. In just eleven appearances, he scored a record-setting seventeen goals. Overall for the season, he scored fifty-one goals in forty-seven appearances, making him Real Madrid's top goal scorer. For the third time in his career, he earned the Pichichi (the award given to the top goal scorer in La Liga) and the European Golden Shoe. Best of all, Ronaldo's wait for his second Ballon d'Or was finally over, as he grabbed the honor away from Lionel Messi. Speaking at the ceremony

Ronaldo received the 2014 FIFA Ballon d'Or award for the player of the year. He received football's highest individual honor for the third time in his career after helping Real Madrid win an unprecedented tenth European Cup/Champions League title.

to pick up his award, his first since joining Real Madrid, a modest Ronaldo seemed genuinely humbled. "I want to become one of the greatest players of all time," he said. "This requires a lot of effort but I hope to get there."[3]

Hoisting the Trophy

Ronaldo and Real Madrid started the 2014 club season in magical form. Threading crossing passes like a seamstress and splitting defenders like paint thinner, Ronaldo broke the Spanish league record of 22 hat tricks shared with another club legend, Alfredo Di Stéfano, by netting three goals in a game against Celta Vigo, on December 6, 2014. That made him the fastest player to reach 200 goals in La Liga, needing only 178 games to get there. Real Madrid set a Spanish league record by

Precious Gifts

After Real Madrid's tenth Champions League title in 2013, Cristiano Ronaldo bought all of his teammates brand-new Bulgari wristwatches, valued at $10,000 apiece. Each watch was engraved with a player's name and "CR7" on one side and the words "La Decima" engraved on the back as a reminder of their collective accomplishment.

Ronaldo also promised Real Madrid's trainers that he would buy a new car for each one, as a gift for helping to keep him fit, if he won the Ballon d'Or later that year. When it was announced that Ronaldo was the best player of 2013 and he was awarded the coveted trophy, Real's training staff also had reason to cheer.

winning 22 games in a row, two wins shy of the world record. Ronaldo scored an incredible 61 goals in 54 appearances and was indisputably the most dominant soccer player in the world. The sport's governing body confirmed as much, awarding him the Ballon d'Or as player of the year for the second straight season, and third time overall.

Continuing to score goals at a record-breaking pace, Ronaldo became Real Madrid's all-time leading scorer, passing Real legend Raúl, by netting his 324th goal as a member of the club, on October 17, 2015. That season, Ronaldo scored 51 goals in 48 appearances, becoming the first player in history to score 50 goals or more in six consecutive seasons. Attesting to the greatness of Ronaldo, his coach, the former Madrid player Zinedine Zidane, said, "When you play with Ronaldo on your team you are already 1–0 up."[4]

Real Madrid fought hard in the La Liga race under new coach Zidane, missing out on the title to archrivals Barcelona by just one point. Nevertheless, Madrid ended its season on a high by reaching the Champions League final, where they would once again face city rival Atlético Madrid in the championship game, in Milan. The game went into the shoot-out stage following a 1–1 draw after extra time. Rising to the dramatic moment, Ronaldo sent the Atlético goalkeeper sprawling the wrong way and converted the decisive penalty kick in the shoot-out to give the Spanish powerhouse a 5-3 victory on penalties. "I knew I would score the winner," said Ronaldo. "I told Zidane to leave me until the last, and everything went well."[5]

For the second time in three years, the biggest game in club soccer ended with Ronaldo ripping off his shirt after victory. Two years earlier, the Portuguese superstar's successful penalty shot had sealed a 4–1 extra-time win over Atlético and prompted the first of his provocative celebrations. Now Real Madrid had won the Champions League title for an unprecedented eleventh time—*La Undécima*—extending the all-time record.

A day after winning the title, Madrid fans filled the Santiago Bernabéu stadium to experience the celebration of La Undécima and enjoy the party along with the players. The celebration began with the stadium in darkness. Images of the eleven European Cup/Champions League trophies were seen on the big screens. Then the lights came on and the players came out one by one to lift the cup toward the Madrid sky with fireworks cascading from the heavens and "We Are The Champions" playing in the background. Ronaldo raised the trophy to the biggest cheer. He scored a record 11 goals in the group stage of the European competition and finished with a total of 16, one short of the record he himself set in 2014. He is the tournament's career leading scorer with 96 goals and is looking to become the first player to score 100 goals in European club competitions. "What I do as an individual only matters if it helps the team win," he said.[6]

Staying Power

Ever since the stunningly disappointing loss on home soil in the title game of the 2004 European Championships,

Ronaldo must have wondered if he would ever bring Portugal so close to major tournament glory again.

The final of the 2016 European Championships pitted Portugal against their French hosts at the Stade de France, just outside Paris. Ronaldo and his teammates were ninety minutes away from bringing home the title that had eluded them and resulted in tears from a teenage Ronaldo twelve years earlier. Now thirty-one, an age when the body usually begins to slow, he envisioned a similar ending, but with a twist. "I hope you'll see me crying tears of joy," he said.[7]

In a cruel twist of fate, Ronaldo's chance at redemption lasted just twenty-four minutes into the final match. That's when Ronaldo left the pitch with a devastating left knee injury, caused by a rough tackle. Crumpled and prone on the turf, Ronaldo slipped off his captain's armband and placed it around a teammate as he was carried on a stretcher to the locker room.

Ronaldo left sobbing as he realized his dream of leading Portugal to European glory was all but over. Yet he quickly returned to the sideline to encourage his teammates. The man once described by many as selfish and individualistic played the role of a true captain and leader by motivating, encouraging, and inspiring his teammates as much as possible from the sideline. "He gave us a lot of confidence and said, 'Listen people, I'm sure we will win, so stay together and fight for it,'"[8] said Portugal's fullback Cedric Soares.

> I wanted to win a trophy with the national team and make history. And I did it.[9]

A rough tackle during the Euro 2016 final match against France left Ronaldo writhing in pain. He was carried away in tears but soon returned to the sideline to encourage his teammates.

• • • • • • • • • • • • • • • • • • • •

Tears of Joy

Faced with the loss of its leader, Portugal did not buckle. Instead, they dug in, carried the match into extra time, and stunned France with a late goal to win the European Championship, 1–0. Ronaldo's tears of despair turned into tears of joy. This emotional win was the first major international trophy for both Ronaldo and Portugal. "It was tough to lose our main man, the man who could at any moment score a goal," the Portuguese defender Pepe said of Ronaldo. "We said we would win it for him and we managed to do that."[10]

At the final whistle, Portugal's players piled on one another in celebration. Once the trophy presentation began, the Portuguese fans never stopped singing their country's anthem. Wearing a knee brace, Ronaldo stepped onto the podium with his team and raised the trophy in triumph. In the locker room after the game, he said, "Forget the individual trophies, Champions League, this one right here is the happiest moment of my life…This is the trophy that was missing."[11]

After bringing a European Championship title to Portugal and another Champions League trophy to Real Madrid, Cristiano Ronaldo ended the year with something just for himself—a fourth world player of the year award. "It was a year that was magnificent at a personal level and at a sporting level," Ronaldo said in his acceptance speech, which he began with "Wow, wow, wow!"[12]

Ronaldo received the Ballon d'Or award a month after his contract with Madrid was extended until 2021, keeping him in Spain until he is thirty-six years old. In addition to countless individual accolades, including five Ballon d'Ors (he again won in 2017), he has so far helped Real Madrid win eight trophies during his time there, including one La Liga title and their historic eleventh Champions League triumph.

A Living Legend

$\cdots\cdots\cdots\cdots\cdots\cdots\cdots\cdots\cdots\cdots\cdots$

W ith one of the most recognizable faces—and torsos—in the world, Cristiano Ronaldo is almost as prolific a pitchman as he is a goal scorer. He is considered to be one of the most handsome men in the entire world, and his iconic image of style and wealth is sought after by scores of prestigious companies looking to promote their products.

The famous good looks are identifiable on an international level, giving the self-confident Ronaldo a swagger that is difficult to ignore. In a book discussing his soccer career, former teammate Wayne Rooney wrote, "In the time I've been playing with Ronnie, the one thing I've noticed about him is that he can't walk past his reflection without admiring it, even if we're about to play a game of football."[1]

Ronaldo has dated a bevy of famous high-profile models, but he has recently settled down with his Spanish girlfiend, Georgina Rodriguez, with whom he had a baby girl, Alana Martina, in November 2017. Ronaldo also had twins via a surrogate mother in June of the same year. The fraternal twins, a girl and a boy, are named Eva Maria and Mateo.

Ronaldo has always tried to keep his private life out of the spotlight and rarely talks about his family. However, it is well known that he is a family man. "My family comes first," he said. "After that, it's the football that matters most to me. Money comes after that."[2]

Expanding His Horizons

Cristiano Ronaldo is the wealthiest and the most popular athlete on the planet. In 2016, the finance magazine *Forbes* rated him the highest-paid athlete in the world at $88 million, including $32 million from endorsements. His Real Madrid contract worth over $50 million a year

Shoe Magnate

In today's world of marketing, it is considered a sign of prestige for an athlete to have his or her own brand of shoe. As part of Cristiano Ronaldo's deal with Nike, the company created a boot called the CR7 line. The Mercurial Superfly CR7 cleats, introduced prior to the 2014 FIFA World Cup, are one of the best-selling soccer shoes on the market. In January 2015, within days of Ronaldo winning the Ballon d'Or, Nike launched the Mercurial Superfly CR7 Rare Gold special edition shoe. The shoes are gold in color and have what are known as "micro-diamonds" fastened and stitched into the shoes.

in salary and bonus runs through 2021, and his Nike agreement, worth $13 million a year until 2020, is the richest endorsement deal in the sport.[3]

Ronaldo's image sells much more than just shoes. He also has endorsement deals with Coca-Cola, Armani clothing, Emirates airline, and watchmaker Tag Heuer, to name a few. His partners are getting their money's worth thanks to Ronaldo's 300 million social media followers across Facebook, Twitter, and Instagram. He became the first athlete with 200 million followers, and his 122 million Facebook fans are more than any other person on the planet.

Ronaldo has expanded his reach by adding a fashion line to his list of projects. Instead of appearing in public in a T-shirt and jeans, as he did when he first went to England, he now prefers dressing more stylishly, wearing designer suits and fitted dress shirts and almost always sporting large diamond earrings. Due to his celebrity status, his fashion style has caught on with other young men who wish to emulate their role model.

In 2014, *Time* magazine named him as one of the one hundred most influential people in the world. He has since opened up his own fashion stores, called CR7, in Funchal and Lisbon that feature fashion accessories designed by Ronaldo himself and other items with a Ronaldo theme. His fashion boutique sells eyeglasses, belt buckles, shoes, dress shirts, underwear, and socks— all marked with the CR7 logo. Ronaldo has his own fragrance, Legacy, in partnership with Eden Parfums, so now his legion of fans will be able to smell just like the five-time world player of the year.

Ronaldo poses beneath a statue of himself during the unveiling ceremony in his hometown of Funchal, Madeira, in 2014. The bronze statue stands over 11 feet (3.3 meters) tall and depicts Ronaldo in his trademark, pre-free-kick stance.

Larger Than Life

In December 2014, a mammoth sculpture of Ronaldo was unveiled in his hometown of Funchal, where twenty years earlier he began to attract attention from professional scouts. The bronze statue stands over 11 feet (3.3 meters) tall and features the Portuguese star in his trademark pre-free-kick stance. The statue is located at Praça do Mar, a square that stretches across the main port entrance of Funchal, where thousands of tourists coming off cruise ships have the opportunity to have their picture taken with the statue of the Real Madrid star.

Nearby is Ronaldo's own personal museum, Museu CR7, which boasts a treasure trove of more than 160 trophies and mementos Ronaldo has won, collectively and individually, during his amazing career. There you will find memorabilia testifying to Ronaldo's talents and achievements: the replica Ballon d'Ors that are lined across the middle of the floor, the replica Golden Boots, the various replica Premier League and Champions League trophies, and a most recent addition, a replica of the Henri Delaunay Cup, the original version of which Ronaldo held aloft at the Stade de France in July 2016 to mark his country's greatest sporting achievement. Museu CR7 features a life-sized wax statue of Ronaldo, and there is also a wax statue of his likeness at the famous Madame Tussauds, a wax museum in London.

"Viva Ronaldo!"

Cristiano Ronaldo's glamorous and wealthy lifestyle bears little resemblance to his humble beginnings on the

102

Sky High

Ronaldo's leaping ability is well documented. In 2013, as a member of Real Madrid, he scored a crucial goal against Manchester United, appearing to hang in the air, defying gravity, as he powered his header into the net. Photographs of the goal showed Ronaldo's knee at the same height as the defender's head as he made contact with the ball. That prompted Museu CR7 to create the "Jump as High as Ronaldo" exhibit, giving fans a chance to leap and try to head a ball dangling from a chord at a height of 9 feet 4 inches (2.84 m).

Portuguese island of Madeira. He went from a poor boy with a tattered soccer ball to now having an international airport named after him. In March 2017, the Madeira airport was officially renamed as Aeroporto Cristiano Ronaldo.

Portugal's president and the prime minister flew to the island and unveiled a commemorative plaque outside the terminal entrance, above a bronze bust of Ronaldo.

There are other reminders of Portugal's greatest living sportsman around the capital city. The Pestana CR7 hotel, in the Chiado district of Lisbon, is no ordinary hotel; it is a living monument to Portugal's most famous citizen. Guests checking in are greeted in the lobby by one of Ronaldo's quotes—"Your love makes me strong, your hate makes me unstoppable"[4]—and a "Viva Ronaldo!" chant is piped through speakers in the corridors.

103

Cristiano Ronaldo flashes his winning smile during a Champions League match in 2017. His famous good looks and confident swagger have made him one of the wealthiest and most popular athletes on the planet.

Highway billboards carrying Ronaldo's image promote everything from mobile telephones to fast food. Images of Ronaldo appear on seemingly every train car on Lisbon's Metro system, so there is no escape from the man whose estimated net worth is over $300 million.

There will likely never again be a player with Ronaldo's combination of strength, athletic ability, and world-renowned image. He is physically fit and capable of playing at a high level for many more years. When he eventually does decide to hang up his soccer cleats and retire, he plans to focus mainly on growing his personal brand. There is no point in making predictions or speculating as to when that day will come, he says, because, "I'm living a dream I never want to wake up from."[5]

Chronology

1985 Cristiano Ronaldo dos Santos Aveiro is born on February 5, in Funchal, the capital city of the Portuguese island of Madeira.

1994 Ronaldo, age nine, joins Andorinha, his first football team in Funchal.

1995 Joins Nacional at ten years old.

1997 At age twelve has a successful tryout with Sporting Lisbon, and the club purchases his contract with Nacional for approximately $27,000, a huge amount for such a young player.

2001 At sixteen is promoted to Sporting Lisbon's senior team, giving him professional status.

2002 On October 7, he scores his first-ever professional goal during his Sporting debut in Primeira Liga against Moreirense; he scores twice in a 3–0 win.

2003 On August 12, Ronaldo signs with Manchester United and becomes the club's first-ever Portuguese player. On August 20, the eighteen-year-old earns his first cap for Portugal in a 1–0 victory over Kazakhstan.

2004 On May 22, Ronaldo scores opening goal in Manchester United's 3–0 win over Millwall in the FA Cup final, his first trophy with MU.

2005 On September 5, Ronaldo's father, Dinis, dies.

2006 Ronaldo and the Portuguese national team defeat England in a Champions League match, causing friction with Manchester United fans.

2007 On May 11, he scores his fiftieth career goal against Manchester City to help Manchester United win its first Premier League title in four years.

2007 Captains Portugal's national team for the first time, at twenty-two. He earns a rare double by winning England's Player of the Year Award and Young Player of the Year Award in the same season.

2008 On May 21, he scores the opening goal against Chelsea as Manchester United wins the Champions League title for a second year in a row. Is given the captain's armband to wear for good

2009 On January 12, he wins FIFA World Player of the Year and the Ballon d'Or for his 2008 season accomplishments. On May 16, he helps United win its third consecutive Premier League title. On July 6, he is introduced at Real Madrid after leaving Manchester United for a record $131 million transfer fee.

2010 On July 3, Ronaldo announces that he has become a father. The baby boy, named Cristiano Junior, is born on June 17. The mother's identity remains unknown.

2011 On April 20, he scores the game-winning goal for Real Madrid in the Copa del Rey final against Barcelona.

2012 On May 13, Ronaldo wins La Liga with Real Madrid.

2013 On December 15, Museu CR7, a museum dedicated to Ronaldo's football career, is opened in his hometown of Funchal.

2014 On January 13, Ronaldo wins his second Ballon d'Or. On May 24, Real Madrid wins its tenth Champions League title, La Decima. On December 21, an 11-foot statue of Ronaldo in his famous free-kick pose is unveiled in his hometown of Funchal, Madeira.

2015 On January 13, he wins his third Ballon d'Or for his exploits in 2014. On September 15, he scores his 500th career goal in a 2–0 victory over Malmo in the Champions League. On October 17, he nets a goal against Levante, his 324th career goal, becoming Real Madrid's all-time leading scorer.

2016 In June, Ronaldo is ranked number 1 on *Forbes*'s list of the world's highest-paid athletes. On July 10, he captains Portugal to its first major international trophy, a 1–0 victory over France, in the final of the European Championships. On December 12, Ronaldo wins his fourth Ballon d'Or, capping a season in which his Portugal side won the European Championship and his club, Real Madrid, took the Champions League.

2017 On March 29, the Madeira Airport is renamed the Cristiano Ronaldo Madeira International Airport. In June, Ronaldo welcomes twins, Eva Maria and Mateo, via a surrogate mother. In November, his girlfriend, Georgina Rodriguez, gives birth to their baby girl, Alana Martina. In the fall, the Portuguese national team qualifies for the 2018 World Cup. On December 7, Ronaldo wins his fifth Ballon d'Or.

Chapter Notes

Introduction

1. Luca Caioli, *Ronaldo: The Obsession for Perfection* (London: Icon Books, 2015), excerpt published in *Goal*, "Teenage Tears and Dreams Demolished: When Cristiano Ronaldo and Portugal Succumbed to Greece at Euro 2004," June 1, 2012, http://www.goal.com/en/news/4240/ronaldo-the-obsession-for-perfection/2012/06/01/3140070/teenage-tears-dreams-demolished-when-cristiano-ronaldo.

Chapter 1: Poor Kid from the Island

1. Luca Caioli, *Ronaldo: The Obsession for Perfection* (London: Icon Books, 2015), p. 5.

2. "Ronaldo Spills All," *Daily Mirror*, July 3, 2011, http://www.mirror.co.uk/3am/celebrity-news/cristiano-ronaldo-spills-all-to-his-close-friend-139054.

3. Ibid.

4. Cristiano Ronaldo, *Moments* (London: Macmillan, 2007), p. 48.

5. "Ronaldo Spills All," *Daily Mirror*.

6. Caioli, p. 11

7. Caioli, p. 15.

Chapter 2: Finding Direction

1. Ben Hayward, "The Making of Cristiano Ronaldo," *Goal*, January 12, 2015, http://www.goal.com/engb/news/3871/ballondor/2015/01/12/7908962/the-making-of-cristiano-ronaldo-how-the-2014-ballon-dor.

2. Luca Caioli, *Ronaldo: The Obsession for Perfection* (London: Icon Books, 2015), p. 13.

3. "Cristiano Ronaldo," Biography Online, http://www.biographyonline.net/sport/football/cristiano-ronaldo.html.

4. Caioli, p. 11.

5. Ibid.

6. Cristiano Ronaldo on Twitter, @TeamCRonaldo, September 14, 2015, https://twitter.com/teamcronaldo/status/643318328774127616.

7. Luca Caioli, *Ronaldo: The Obsession for Perfection* (London: Icon Books, 2015), excerpt published in *Goal*, "Teenage Tears and Dreams Demolished: When Cristiano Ronaldo and Portugal Succumbed to Greece at Euro 2004," June 1, 2012, http://www.goal.com/en/news/4240/ronaldo-the-obsession-for-perfection/2012/06/01/3140070/teenage-tears-dreams-demolished-when-cristiano-ronaldo.

8. Ibid.

9. Caioli, *Ronaldo: The Obsession for Perfection*, p. 14.

Chapter 3: From Madeira to Portugal

1. Luca Caioli, *Ronaldo: The Obsession for Perfection* (London: Icon Books, 2015), p. 16.

2. Ibid.

3. Caioli, p. 19.

4. Ed Malyon, "Ronaldo Prepared for Special Clash," *Daily Mirror*, September 14, 2016, http://www.irishmirror.ie/sport/soccer/soccer-news/cristiano-ronaldo-prepared-special-clash-8830413.

5. Cristiano Ronaldo on Facebook, July 7, 2011, https://www.facebook.com/PassionCristianoRonaldo/posts/226295507404316.

6. Ibid.

7. Cristiano Ronaldo, *Moments* (London: Macmillan, 2007), p. 56.

8. Cristiano Ronaldo on Facebook, July 7, 2011, https://www.facebook.com/PassionCristianoRonaldo/posts/226295507404316.

9. Alberto Pinero, "Ronaldo Cried for Days After Joining Sporting," *Goal*, September 13, 2006, http://www.goal.com/en-gb/news/2565/exclusive/2016/09/13/27451822/ronaldo-cried-for-days-after-joining-sporting-reveals-the?ICID=HP_BN_10.

10. Cristiano Ronaldo, *Moments* (London: Macmillan, 2007), p. 56.

11. Guillem Balague, *Cristiano Ronaldo: The Biography* (London: Orion, 2015).

12. Caioli, p. 21.

13. Caioli, p. 35.

14. Ibid.

Chapter 4: A Fresh Start

1. "Manchester United Winger Cristiano Ronaldo Needed Heart Operation to Save Career," *Telegraph*, January 29, 2009, http://www.telegraph.co.uk/ sport/football/players/cristiano-ronaldo/4382937/ Manchester-United-winger-Cristiano-Ronaldo- needed-heart-operation-to-save-career.html.

2. "Made in Sporting: Lisbon Club's Youth Academy Sets it Apart," *New York Times*, Rory Smith, November 21, 2016, https://www.nytimes.com/2016/11/21/sports/ soccer/soccer-sporting-lisbon-youth-academy.html?_ r=0.

3. Guillem Balague, *Cristiano Ronaldo: The Biography* (London: Orion, 2015).

4. Cristiano Ronaldo, *Moments* (London: Macmillan, 2007), p. 23.

5. Luca Caioli, *Ronaldo: The Obsession for Perfection* (London: Icon Books, 2015), p. 38.

6. Ibid.

Chapter 5: Playing for a Living

1. John Naughton, "How Cristiano Ronaldo Became the Best in the World," *Men's Health*, June 23, 2016, http:// www.menshealth.co.uk/fitness/sports-training/how- cristiano-ronaldo-became-the-best-in-the-world.

2. Associated Press, "United Land Other Ronaldo," *Guardian*, August 12, 2003, https://www.theguardian. com/football/2003/aug/12/newsstory.sportinglisbon.

3. Ibid.

4. Dan Taylor, "Teenager Takes Beckham No. 7 Shirt," *Guardian*, August 13, 2003, http://www.theguardian. com/football/2003/aug/13/newsstory.sport10.

5. Associated Press, "United Land Other Ronaldo," *Guardian*, August 12, 2003, https://www.theguardian. com/football/2003/aug/12/newsstory.sportinglisbon.

6. Quoted in BBC documentary, *Sir Alex Ferguson: Secrets of Success*, *Daily Mirror*, October 7, 2015, http://www.mirror.co.uk/sport/football/news/ cristiano-ronaldo-reveals-sir-alex-6592110.

7. Tom Oldfield, *Cristiano Ronaldo: The Inside Story of the Greatest Footballer on Earth* (London: John Blake, 2007), p. 23.

8. Luca Caioli, *Ronaldo: The Obsession for Perfection* (London: Icon Books, 2015), p. 46.

9. Cristiano Ronaldo, *Moments* (London: Macmillan, 2007), p. 23.

10. Oldfield, p. 33.

11. Ibid.

12. Justyn Barnes, "Man United Legend George Best on Cristiano Ronaldo's Debut," *Sabotage Times*, Sept. 15, 2014, http://sabotagetimes.com/football/man-united-legend-george-best-on-cristiano-ronaldos-debut.

Chapter 6: The Changing World

1. Rob Beasley, "Ronaldo: Every Goal Is Dedicated to My Dad," *Sun*, May 29, 2014, https://www.thesun.co.uk/archives/football/850663/ronaldo-every-goal-is-dedicated-to-my-dad/.

2. Ibid.

3. "Rooney 'Gobsmacked' by Red Card," BBC News, July 3, 2006, http://news.bbc.co.uk/sport2/hi/football/world_cup_2006/5141510.stm.

4. Ibid.

5. Ibid.

6. "Most Hated Man in Britain to Get Frosty Reception at Home," *Manchester Evening News*, September 5, 2007, http://www.manchestereveningnews.co.uk/news/local-news/most-hated-man-in-britain-to-get-frosty-1037047.

7. "Man U to Sack Ronaldo," *Sydney Morning Herald*, July 3, 2006, http://www.smh.com.au/news/football/man-u-to-sack-ronaldo-report/2006/07/03/1151778867128.html.

8. Associated Press, "Rooney Is Given Two-Match Ban," *Los Angeles Times*, July 9, 2006, http://articles.latimes.com/2006/jul/09/sports/sp-cupnotes9.

9. Cristiano Ronaldo on Facebook, July 7, 2011, https://www.facebook.com/PassionCristianoRonaldo/posts/226295214071012.

10. Joe Ridge, "Is Ronaldo the Best Header of a Ball in World Football?" *Daily Mail*, July 7, 2016, http://www.dailymail.co.uk/sport/euro2016/article-3678637/

After-towering-winner-against-Wales-Euro-2016-
semi-final-Cristiano-Ronaldo-best-header-ball-
world-football.html.

11. Justyn Barnes, "Man United Legend George Best on
Cristiano Ronaldo's Debut," *Sabotage Times*, Sept. 15,
2014, http://sabotagetimes.com/football/man-united-
legend-george-best-on-cristiano-ronaldos-debut.

Chapter 7: Cristiano's Big Move

1. Steve Wilson, "Sir Alex Ferguson 'Wouldn't Sell
Real Madrid a Virus', Let Alone Cristiano Ronaldo,"
Telegraph, December 18, 2008, http://www.
telegraph.co.uk/sport/football/teams/manchester-
united/3832913/Sir-Alex-Ferguson-wouldnt-sell-
Real-Madrid-a-virus-let-alone-Cristiano-Ronaldo.
html.

2. Paul Logothetis, "80,000 Fans Welcome Ronaldo to
Real Madrid," *San Diego Union Tribune*, July 6, 2009,
http://www.sandiegouniontribune.com/sdut-soc-real-
madrid-ronaldo-070609-2009jul06-story.html.

3. "Ronaldo Welcomed by 80,000 Fans at Real Madrid
Unveiling" *Guardian*, July 6, 2009, https://www.
theguardian.com/football/2009/jul/06/cristiano-
ronaldo-real-madrid-bernabeu.

4. Tom Williams, "Portugal's Ronaldo Dedicates Goals to
Son," *Mail & Guardian*, June 18, 2012, https://mg.co.
za/article/2012-06-18-ronaldo-dad-euro-2012.

5. Gordon Tynan, "Mourinho: Ronaldo Is Best Player in
the Universe," *Independent*, October 12, 2012, http://
www.independent.co.uk/sport/football/european/

mourinho-ronaldo-is-the-best-player-in-the-universe-8209775.html.

6. "Ronaldo: Rivalry with Messi Motivates Both Players," ESPNFC.com, January 20, 2015, http://www.espnfc. us/spanish-primera-division/story/2254941/cristiano-ronaldo-says-rivalry-with-lionel-messi-motivates-both-players.

7. "Ronaldo Takes Aim at Sepp Blatter After Hairdresser Remark," *Guardian*, October 29, 2013, https://www. theguardian.com/football/2013/oct/29/real-madrid-sepp-blatter-cristiano-ronaldo-hairdresser.

8. Jaime Uribarri, "Ronaldo: I'm Better Than Messi," *New York Daily News*, May 18, 2012, http://www. nydailynews.com/blogs/the-beautiful-blog/cristiano-ronaldo-better-lionel-messi-blog-entry-1.1626305.

9. Paul Wilson, "I Have Nothing Left to Prove," *Guardian*, May 17, 2008, https://www.theguardian. com/football/2008/may/18/manchesterunited. championsleague.

10. "I'm Rich, Handsome and a Great Player," BBC Sport, September 15, 2011, http://www.bbc.com/sport/football/14928049.

Chapter 8: Portugal's Great Hope

1. Igor Mladenovic, "Ronaldo: I Will Only Reach the Top When I Win a Trophy with Portugal," *Goal*, May 26, 2012, http://www.goal.com/en/news/2898/euro-2012/2012/05/26/3127044/cristiano-ronaldo-i-will-only-reach-the-top-when-i-win-a.

2. Tim Lewis, "Ronaldo" He's Got God-Given Talent, and He Knows It," *Guardian*, November 23, 2013, https://www.theguardian.com/theobserver/2013/nov/24/cristiano-ronaldo-real-madrid-portugal-football.

3. Andy Brassell, "The Night Ronaldo Ran Away with the Ballon d'Or," *Guardian*, November 20, 2013, https://www.theguardian.com/football/blog/2013/nov/20/cristiano-ronaldo-ballon-dor-portugal-world-cup-2014.

4. *Football Espana*, "Mou in Amazing Defence of Ronaldo," October 12, 2012, http://www.football-espana.net/24919/mou-amazing-defence-ronaldo.

5. "Cristiano Ronaldo," Biography Online, http://www.biographyonline.net/sport/football/cristiano-ronaldo.html.

6. Ibid.

7. Kevin Baxter, "Charity Is Nothing New for Ronaldo," *Los Angeles Times*, May 17, 2014, http://www.latimes.com/sports/la-sp-wc-cristiano-ronaldo-20140518-story.html

Chapter 9: Guts and Glory

1. Mark Ogden, "Ronaldo's Homecoming Party Passes Him By as Real Madrid See off Sporting," ESPNFC, November 22, 2016, http://www.espnfc.us/blog/the-match/60/post/3001023/cristiano-ronaldo-homecoming-party-passes-him-by-as-real-madrid-see-off-sporting.

2. Jamie Jackson, "Ronaldo Sad After His Goal Knocks Out Manchester United," *Guardian*, March 6, 2013,

https://www.theguardian.com/football/2013/mar/06/
cristiano-ronaldo-manchester-united-real-madrid.

3. "Ronaldo Retains Ballon d'Or," Eurosport.com,
December 1, 2015, http://www.eurosport.com/
football/ronaldo-retains-ballon-d-or_sto4544508/
story.shtml.

4. Sagnik Kundu, "10 Best Quotes on Ronaldo,"
Sportskeeda, February 24, 2017, https://www.
sportskeeda.com/football/10-best-quotes-cristiano-
ronaldo.

5. "Knew I'd Score the Winner: Ronaldo," *Telegraph*, May
30, 2016, https://www.telegraphindia.com/1160530/
jsp/sports/story_88413.jsp#.WOcjAVKZPuQ.

6. Eduardo Correia and Pedro C. Garcia, "The
Unexpected Life of Cristiano Ronaldo," Portugal Daily
View, June 27, 2012, http://www.portugaldailyview.
com/whats-new/cristiano-ronaldo-the-humble-
chosen-one.

7. Sky Sports, "Ronaldo Hoping for Tears of Joy
After Firing Portugal to Euro 2016 Final," July
7, 2016, http://www.skysports.com/football/
news/13954/10481660/cristiano-ronaldo-hoping-for-
tears-of-joy-after-firing-portugal-to-euro-2016-final.

8. Miguel Delaney, "Ronaldo's Unbelievable Halftime
Speech Inspired Portugal," ESPNFC, July 10, 2016,
http://www.espnfc.us/european-championship/
story/2911135/euro-2016-cristiano-ronaldo-gave-
unbelievable-speech-to-in-shock-portugal-soares.

9. "Ronaldo: No One Believed in Us," Fox Sports Asia, July 11, 2016, http://www.foxsportsasia.com/news/ronaldo-no-one-believed-in-us/.

10. Teddy Cutler, "Pepe: Portugal Won Euro 2016 for Ronaldo," *Newsweek*, July 11, 2016, http://www.newsweek.com/cristiano-ronaldo-portugal-euro-2016-sport-479382.

11. Jamie Spencer, "Ronaldo's Touching Dressing Room Speech After Euro Win," Yahoo Sports, November 19, 2016, https://uk.sports.yahoo.com/news/video-incredible-footage-released-ronaldos-093656485.html.

12. Graham Dunbar, "Cristiano Ronaldo, Carli Lloyd Win FIFA Best Player Awards," *Boston Herald*, January 9, 2017, https://www.reviewjournal.com/sports/cristiano-ronaldo-carli-lloyd-win-fifa-best-player-awards/.

Chapter 10: A Living Legend

1. Jay Jaffa, "Ronaldo Can't Walk Past His Reflection Without Admiring It Says Rooney," *Goal*, September 9, 2012, http://www.goal.com/en-gb/news/2896/premier-league/2012/09/09/3363769/ronaldo-cant-walk-past-his-reflection-without-admiring-it.

2. "The Real Cristiano Ronaldo: What Matters to Me? Family, Football, Money," *Daily Mirror*, July 2, 2011, http://www.mirror.co.uk/sport/football/news/exclusive-interview---real-cristiano-3323351.

3. Kurt Badenhausen, "Ronaldo Generates $176 Million in Value for His Sponsors on Social Media," *Forbes*, June 8, 2016, https://www.forbes.com/sites/

kurtbadenhausen/2016/06/08/ronaldo-generates-176-million-in-value-for-his-sponsors-on-social-media/#713ad5d77234.

4. Cristiano Ronaldo on Twitter, @TeamCRonaldo, March 25, 2015, https://twitter.com/teamcronaldo/status/580768955226152962?lang=en.

5. Cristiano Ronaldo on Twitter, @TeamCRonaldo, October 19, 2015, https://twitter.com/teamcronaldo/status/656310519696109568.

Glossary

Ballon d'Or Award presented by FIFA (Fédération Internationale de Football Association) to the best player of the year.

bicycle kick A volley out of the air in which the player kicks the ball over his own head.

caps In British sport, a metaphorical term for a player's appearance in a game at international level. The term dates from the practice in the United Kingdom of awarding a cap to every player in an international match of association football.

friendly A match between two teams that has no importance in the standings of either.

gobsmacked British slang term that means extremely shocked.

nil Zero, especially as a score in a game.

paparazzi Photographers that pursue celebrities and take intrusive pictures for newspapers and magazines.

phenomenon An extraordinary occurrence or circumstance.

philanthropist A person who promotes the well-being of humanity, usually by charitable donation or action.

pitch A playing field.

prodigy A young person endowed with exceptional qualities and abilities.

tackle To use the feet to forcefully get the ball away from an opposing player who has it.

transfer fee The amount of money a sports team pays to another team in order to purchase a player from that team.

treble To become three times greater, or to triple.

truancy The act of being absent without permission.

viva An expression that means "long live"; used to express support.

World Cup A soccer tournament held every four years in which qualifying national teams compete to determine a world champion.

Further Reading

Books

Balague, Guillem. *Cristiano Ronaldo: The Biography.* London, UK: Orion Publishing Group, 2016.

Caioli, Luca. *Ronaldo: The Obsession for Perfection.* London, UK: Icon Books, 2017.

Part, Michael. *Cristiano Ronaldo: The Rise of a Winner.* Beverly Hills, CA: Sole Books, 2014.

Stewart, Gail B. *Cristiano Ronaldo* (People in the News). San Diego, CA: Lucent Books, 2015.

Websites

Cristiano Ronaldo's Official Website

http://www.cristianoronaldo.com

Site contains statistics, photographs, and a career timeline.

Cristiano Ronaldo's Fan Page

http://www.ronaldo7.net

Chat rooms where fans discuss everything Ronaldo; also has biographical information.

Real Madrid Club de Fútbol

http://www.realmadrid.com/en/football/squad/cristiano-ronaldo-dos-santos

Player profile of star player Cristiano Ronaldo.

Films

Cristiano Ronaldo: The World at His Feet. Dir. Tara Pirnia. Stax Entertainment, 2014.

Ronaldo. Dir. Anthony Wonke. On The Corner Films, 2015.

Ronaldo: Tested to the Limit, Dir. Mike McDowall. Plum Pictures, 2011.

Index